The State of
EQUALITY
in the Equality State

Saving the Best of the West in Wyoming

Paul Jensen

www.pronghornpress.org

For all the immigrants to Wyoming, who were newcomers then and built the state's ranches, towns, and cities, and to the new generation of newcomers or immigrants who hold the state's future in their hands.

Acknowledgments

Many believe that a second book will be easier to write than the first. While the writing was easier, this book was very different and more demanding. So I would like to thank my wife, Sherrill, and my youngest daughter, Lily, for their patience and support.

Next, I would like to recognize and thank Annette Chaudet, editor and owner of Pronghorn Press, who has published both of my books and made each so much better.

I would also like to thank Albert and Sue Sommers and Victor and Jo Mack, who read earlier drafts of the book, and improved it.

I would like to thank Nikki Mann for graciously making available a photo from her and Andy Nelson's book, *Jonah,* a beautiful collection of photos and cowboy poetry. That photo of Sublette County cowboy, Brian Bjornsen, became the cover of this book. I would also thank Brian for giving his permission to use the photo.

Table of Contents

1

State Pride

Saving the Best of the West in Wyoming

Before moving to Wyoming six years ago, I lived in and visited a number of states. I was born in Denver, Colorado, on September 26, 1946. I then moved with my family to Ames, Iowa; Lexington, Kentucky; West Lafayette, Indiana; and Roseville, Minnesota where I attended junior high school, high school, and college. After college graduation, I moved to Washington, D.C., and attended graduate school. That began a thirty year career in the nation's capitol working in national politics, government, and as a founding partner of a public relations company. Along the way, I have also spent more than a few days working in New Hampshire, Massachusetts, North Carolina, Georgia, Florida, Texas, Illinois, Michigan, and California.

In each of the states where I lived with my parents and siblings, we met the prevailing popular culture and the pride that residents felt about the state's attributes, natural beauty, and historical highlights. It didn't matter whether these views about popular culture and history were true or longstanding myths. Eager to find acceptance in a new city and state, we didn't question them either. Most people don't, and almost none take the time to discover or discern the difference between folklore or myths and their real foundation of state pride.

For example, Minnesota has long fostered the image of the "Land of 10,000 Lakes" where nature is wild and undisturbed—a place dominated by small rural towns settled by Scandinavian or German immigrants. Paraphrasing Garrison Keillor from *Prairie Home Companion* and "his mythical" *Lake Wobegon*—it is a place where "all the women are good looking and all children above average." Suburban and exurban sprawl, many residents now from out of state, lakeside homes, dying lakes, and the gentrification of smaller mining towns in northeastern Minnesota, such as Ely, have pulled the mask from the face of this myth. For example, the 2.85 million residents of the seven county Twin Cities area account for 55% of the state's entire population. Maintaining its edge in the world of mall shopping, Minnesota's most recent entrant, Mall of America in Bloomington, Minnesota, is the size of 78 football fields. The 2007 Minnesota National Lakes Project, conducted jointly by the Environmental Protection Agency and the Minnesota Pollution Control Agency, found a concentration of a virulent blue-green algae toxin "above detection levels" in 56% of the sample lakes. Another 27% were above the World Health Association's drinking water standard, and one of the fifty sample lakes was so toxic that boaters, fishermen, and swimmers were advised not to use the lake.

But the citizens of Minnesota are not alone in persisting in a belief that is belied by facts. Most people are simply comfortable with and prideful about their state and its prevailing myths.

Until my wife, Sherrill, ten-year old daughter, Lily, and I moved to Wyoming, we were no more engaged in our states' histories than most others. However, when we moved to Wyoming our perspective changed. We were tired of big city congestion, polluted air, insufferable heat and humidity, and the contentious atmosphere of living every day with millions of people, cars, and trucks. We wanted the big vistas, the open space, wildlife, the mountains, the seasons, and outdoor adventures of Wyoming. We wanted to know its history, cowboy legacy, and way of life. We learned them from experience, research, horseback conversations, skiing, writing a book, and friends.

However, since we have lived in many states and different cultures, Sherrill and I could compare our new life with other ways of living. While appreciating the state and its attributes that drew us here in the first place, we could also see the limitations and the imperfections in how residents viewed the state. Our state pride and the confounding myths have led to this book, *The State of Equality in the Equality State: Saving the Best of the West in Wyoming.*

In chapters of this book I have exposed some of the state's most cherished myths, but by telling the truth, I have also unveiled what is most appealing about Wyoming and what will be necessary to grow and preserve it. While the first chapters may cause the most ardent Wyomingites some indigestion, the literary trip through the whole book will be as refreshing as an antacid.

I have also created a framework or template for other authors or filmmakers to examine the states where they live. I can envision a series on different states. Those explorations of state culture, lore, and the real world cannot only dispel debilitating myths, but can also bring forth entertainment and a road map to a better future.

2

Wyoming:
You're So Square
(Baby, I Don't Care)

Saving the Best of the West in Wyoming

If you are a student of rock and roll or came of age in the 1950s, you may remember this song. Its first verse may be even more familiar:

> *You don't like crazy music*
> *You don't like rockin' bands*
> *You just want to go the movie show*
> *And sit there holdin' hands*
> *You're so square*
> *Baby I don't care*

If this song strikes a chord, you still probably don't know that it was specifically written for Elvis Presley by leading song writers and producers, Jerry Leiber and Mike Stoller. In April, 1957, during their first recording session with Elvis, Leiber and Stoller also produced *Jail House Rock* and *Treat Me Nice*. However, *You're So Square* became a more standard song sung by Buddy Holly and later by Joni Mitchell.

Saving the Best of the West in Wyoming

This song perfectly captures life in Wyoming, and although my family and I and are "newcomers," squareness touches everybody. As we will learn very shortly, the state is just off center. Its culture, mannerisms, and social life are a little off-beat.

As a matter of geography, boundaries, and surveys, Wyoming is so square, too—not precisely square, but square enough. The state, nicknamed the Equality State, the Big Wonderful, or the Cowboy State is ninety-nine miles longer than it is wide. From east to west its boundaries lie 375 miles apart and from north to south the boundaries are 276 miles apart. Since Wyoming was laid out along the lines of latitude and longitude, it has four straight edges and four right angles. That gets us closer to square.

Remember that when looking at a map, latitude lines run horizontally. Latitude lines are also known as parallels and are an equal distance from each other. Each degree of latitude is approximately sixty-nine miles from the next, and zero degree marks the Equator. The North Pole is ninety degrees north and the South Pole is ninety degrees south. Since zero degrees latitude is fixed and can be roughly gauged by the length of the day or the height of the sun, early sailors and explorers, such as Christopher Columbus, could navigate only using the lines of latitude.

Since the distance between degrees of longitude change from the Equator where one degree equals sixty miles to the poles where it equals almost nothing, locating lines of longitude took several more centuries and an English

clockmaker, John Harrison, to accurately
calculate. Zero degrees longitude is located
in Greenwich, England. However, Wyoming's
boundaries of latitude and longitude were
drawn in reference to Washington, D.C., so its
western boundary is about two and a half
miles off from where it should be. From the very
beginning Wyoming was just a little bit off, and
that gave "square" another meaning, and that is
"odd" or just off-key or culturally out-of-tune with
other Western states if not, the rest of the country.

Unlike most states whose boundaries are
defined mainly or in part by coasts, rivers, valleys,
and divides, Wyoming is one of only three states
whose boundaries are only defined by lines of
latitude and longitude. The other two states are
Colorado and Utah, and Colorado is the only other
"square" state. Its length or its east to west
boundary is also about a hundred miles longer
than its north to south boundary, but again it has
the straight edges and angles of Wyoming, and it
was laid out in reference to Washington, D.C., too.

When Wyoming's territorial status was
finalized on May 19, 1869, it was drawn primarily
from the western Dakota Territory and squared
out from small portions of Idaho and Utah. In all
likelihood these boundaries were established
along those specific lines of latitude and longitude
because surveyors and lawmakers did not need
a detailed knowledge of the land to create the
Wyoming Territory or other western territories.
Further, some speculate that when the western
territories, and then states, were laid out, the U.S.
Congress tried to avoid ill-will and controversy

among western states by creating states of roughly equal size. Accordingly, Wyoming and Colorado may have been cut square to make other western states "fit" and still end up with western states about the same size.

When on July 10, 1890, Wyoming became a state, its territorial boundaries were used to define those of the state. As written in Article 11, Section 1 of the state's Constitution, the borders are defined as:

Commencing at the intersection of the twenty-seventh meridian of longitude west from Washington with the forty-fifth degree of north latitude; thence south to the forty-first degree north latitude; thence east to the twenty-seventh meridian of west longitude; thence north the place of beginning.

This section of any state Constitution can really get your blood flowing.

Be There and Be Square

Of course, since there are only two "square states," and square states are unique in more ways than one, living in one is also unique. My wife, Sherrill, and youngest daughter, Lily, and I have been uniquely square for six years. We moved from Washington, D.C., which is not a state, and we now live in ranch country near Daniel, Wyoming.

Today, we join 532,665 other Wyomingites inhabiting these 97,884 square miles. That means we have 5.4 persons per square mile. In some parts of the state you can still drive for miles and not see another person.

Travel has been and still is measured by time not distance. Wyoming is the least populated state in the country. However, about 46% of the state's land is owned by the federal government.

It is estimated that sagebrush covers about half of Wyoming's land, and unless you live here, that fact may create images of desolation. But many of today's Wyoming residents realize that the sagebrush ocean that once occupied 150 million acres—half of the American West—is rapidly disappearing. Since sagebrush habitats are home to 350 associated plant and animal species, including the sage grouse, they are threatened, too.

However, there is no denying that we do have plenty of space *where seldom is heard a discouraging word and the deer and the antelope play,* and play they do. We share our space with 564,580 pronghorns, 521,070 mule deer, 102,281 elk, at least 600 grizzly bears and a mere 10,154 moose, 1,085 buffalo, and 302 wolves. Beyond those animals and on the 53,750 square miles of privately owned ranchland, we are neighbors to 1.44 million head of cattle.

These numbers translate into 3 head of cattle per person, one antelope per person, almost 1 mule deer per person, not even close to 1 elk per person, and almost no grizzly bears, moose, bison, or wolves on a per capita basis.

We are the Big Wonderful—or at least so think the wildlife and beef cattle that share our space. Let's look at how some others in the state describe it. One of my personal favorites has been the state tourism slogan, *Forever, Wyoming.*

Of course, *forever* is a very long time, and what were we preserving forever? Was it our economy's dependence on energy production, our failure to diversify our economy, the out-migration of our young people, or the inequality of income between men and women?

The slogan referred to the wide-open spaces and the blue sunlit sky of Wyoming, but like many others, it prefers to ignore or obscure the other Wyoming that is just a little out-of-step.

In the early summer of 2008, and with no fanfare, Wyoming tourism changed its slogan to *Forever, West.* Since Wyoming will forever lie in the Rocky Mountain West, I can't quibble with the new tagline.

Another tagline that just rolls off the tongue and creates vivid images of Western life is the one concocted by the Jackson Hole Chamber of Commerce—*Respecting the Power of Place.* When I imagine power of place, I first think about a magnet that attracts the thousands of new residents and tourists who have dramatically changed the character of Jackson. Next, I think of the power of money that is required to purchase the average Jackson home. Now it is a cool $1.363 million with the least expensive, a one bedroom town house, priced at an affordable $540,000. That's the real power of place, and it deserves some grudging respect.

Since Sheridan, Wyoming, still has King Rope, the Mint Bar, the Big Horns, and a few historic ranches, I like the simplicity and directness of its tagline, *The Best of the West.* I am also a fan of the Cowboy Shop's line, *STILL WESTERN after all these years.* The Cowboy Shop, an authentic Western store, is located in Pinedale, Wyoming, about seventy miles south of Jackson, and it is owned and managed by Bob and Carolyn Bing, who also carry my books.

The appeal of these taglines lies in their direct reference to Western life and a connection to elements of the West that are still very real. They are simple and understandable, and neither tries to say too much or over-promises. In a later chapter, *Newcomers and Old Timers,* the reader will find a longer discussion of this proposition.

Since this chapter reveals that Wyoming is square in more ways than one and somewhat out of tune, a short road map to the rest of the collection can aid the reader. The City of Cheyenne, the state capitol, has a slogan known as *Living the Legend.* Wyoming has many legends and legendary people. Some of it is true and a few, who populate its history, are truly legendary, but some of it is just a long stretch of the imagination. Whether it is the Equality State, place names, native Wyomingites versus newcomers or the Cowboy State, these chapters will dig into the lore and myths. Digging will expose new truths and yet confirm the pristine nature of Wyoming, its real attraction, and its future.

3

The Equality State

Saving the Best of the West in Wyoming

Although the *Big Wonderful* still sneaks in as a state nickname, the major league competition is between the *Equality State* and the *Cowboy State*. Which one most accurately depicts the culture and vision of Wyoming? Reflecting the fact that no one in Wyoming wants to choose or have reality impinge on state myths, the symbol of each stands together on the Wyoming state quarter officially issued in early September, 2007.

First adopted by Wyoming's Second Legislature in 1893, the Wyoming State Seal featured a woman in the center, who had a banner proclaiming "EQUAL RIGHTS." The banner commerates the near revolutionary act of December 10, 1869, when Wyoming's very first territorial legislature gave women full voting rights and the right to hold elected office. At that time, no other government in the world had given women those rights.

However, in the euphoria of the past and

present, Wyoming forgot that just one year later, in 1870, and for wholly different reasons, Utah Territory gave women the right to vote. Although Wyoming and Utah were remarkably different in culture and religion, they were similar in that neither had a suffrage society, any divisive political partisanship in their one party legislatures or any visible indication that women wanted or demanded the franchise. The women in both territories were handed the right to vote on the proverbial "silver platter."

Since women in Utah Territory and Washington Territory temporarily lost their franchise around 1887, for a few years Wyoming was the only territory and state (1890) where women had the right to vote and hold office. However, by 1896, the states of Wyoming, Colorado (1893), Utah (1896) and Idaho (1896) all had bestowed voting rights on their women citizens, and in 1896, they were the only four suffrage states in the country.

The suffrage map of 1914 showed that all states from the Rocky Mountains west, except New Mexico, had given women the right to vote. No state east of the Rockies, except Kansas, had done so. Yet, all of the better known and active suffragists such as, Susan B. Anthony, Elizabeth Cady Stanton, Lucy Stone, and Henry B. Blackwell, lived in the East.

Returning to the state seal that stands for the authority and sovereignty of the State of Wyoming, we find two men standing to the left and right of the woman with the banner, and they represent the livestock and mining industries. Next, a five-pointed star highlights Wyoming's admission to the Union as the forty-fourth state, but on top of the pillars rest lamps from which burn the Light of Knowledge.

This chapter, the *Equality State,* will let that "light of knowledge" shine on the myth of equality in Wyoming, and on the story of how and why the franchise of voting rights for women was first awarded in Wyoming Territory. This light can also illuminate the *Equality State's* treatment of minorities and others who have faced discrimination and inequality.

Nine-to-Five

According to the most recent and complete Census Bureau's American Community Survey for Wyoming, in 2006, the median earnings of the 67,007 full-time working women hit $27,926. That compares to the median earnings of $41,913 for the 107,890 full-time working men. Annually, Wyoming women earn $13,387 less than men or only 67 cents for each dollar earned by a man.

Comparable data for the United States shows that women earn $32,649 or $9,651 less than men. That means a woman in the United States makes 77 cents for each dollar earned by a man.

For a more neighborly comparison let's peek first at the other square state, Colorado. A full time working woman in Colorado makes 80 cents for every dollar earned by a man, and in the Cornhusker State she makes 78 cents. Even in Montana, a woman makes 72 cents for every dollar made by a man.

If a Wyoming woman has an advanced degree—a graduate or professional degree—she will make 74 cents for every dollar made by her male counterpart. That means a woman, who may be a doctor, registered nurse, a lawyer, or university professor, will make less than 75% of a professional man's income.

The final snapshot of inequality shows that 25% more Wyoming women live in poverty than Wyoming men.

Although statistics can sometimes jumble the mind, no matter how you slice the facts, Wyoming working women make considerably less than their male counterparts, and usually that differential is worse than the national earnings profile comparing men and women. Even more illuminating is the fact that the earnings gap between Wyoming men and women is much, much greater than the gap between men and women in three of Wyoming's neighboring states.

Now hardly surprising, Wyoming working women's median earnings of $27,926 rank them forty-third in the country where women in the District of Columbia, who made $48,586, are ranked first.

History Works, Too

The first obvious question is how did the myth of equality so totally eclipse the facts? As we shall see, this came about through a romanticized history. But the real story is much more interesting than the fantasized version. So let's climb aboard Mr. Peabody's time machine and witness Wyoming's territorial life around 1869.

As we come out of time warp, the magnitude, aridity, and clarity of Western space and the near complete absence of people sears that first sight into our minds. No wonder that a special census in June and July, 1869, counted a population of only 8,014. By 1870, the population swelled to 9,118 or just about one person every ten square miles.

The transcontinental ribbon of rails known as the Union Pacific never attracted the 35,000 new residents it had promised. Instead, it served as a bridge across Wyoming to richer, more fertile, and hospitable country.

In 1870, the Census also showed that Wyoming had only three hundred paid working women compared to 6,345 men.

In 1869, walking along any dirt or muddy street in any of the eight Wyoming towns with 300 or more people, we are joined by cows, pigs, dogs and other assorted livestock.

It seems that from almost every other door wafts the smell of stale beer and cigarette smoke. Each door opens into a saloon with patrons streaming in and out, day or night. We find gambling games of poker, keno, roulette, and dice at tables in every saloon. Often customers rush outside with greenbacks in their hands and wager hundreds of dollars on a horse race down the main street.

Cheyenne's population of 1,450 were served by 27 saloonkeepers, 4 brewers, 3 liquor store clerks, and 2 tobacco and liquor merchants. Even South Pass City, a short lived gold mining town and an odd mecca for a few Wyoming suffragists, by the early 1870s, had just 460 residents, but boasted 7 retail liquor dealers, 3 brewers, and 1 wholesale liquor dealer.

In a toast to those workers, the 1870 Census confirmed that selling drinks remained the major service industry in Wyoming.

Drinking and the rowdy bar life drew a predominately male crowd. Coal miners, soldiers, railroad workers, and freighters, drank just as hard as the cowboys, but more often. Most survived, but everyone drank his share of bad whisky and beer.

Hand in glove with the disproportionate number of single men came prostitution, a licensed business at the time. The madams' houses sprang up along the rail lines and near military forts. Many of these whorehouses were known as "hog ranches." They were started as pig or hog farms to provide a steady supply of pork to the forts or rail workers. More transient men and women were hired by these farms. In such isolated surroundings, the women started "serving double duty" to the soldiers and others, and they were well paid. As a growing supply of beef began to replace pork in soldier and railroad worker diets, many hog ranches could no longer compete and became brothels.

In the 1870s, it was estimated that Wyoming had over 300 prostitutes—1 for every 70 residents. Since prostitution was not an occupation listed in the U.S Census, most estimates are more guesswork than fact. The estimate of 300 ladies of the night was drawn from J.H. Beadle's 1881 edition of his book, *Western Wilds and the Men Who Redeemed Them* and cited in T.A Larson's *History of Wyoming.*

We do know that prostitution was prevalent and visible. For example, many merchants feared losing business to other cities if their towns failed to provide prostitutes for cowboys, railroad workers, loggers, and freighters.

Heavy drinking, gambling, prostitution, and

ill-mannered living underscored the second most striking characteristic of territorial Wyoming, namely the scarcity of women. In 1870, there were 6 men 21 years old or older for every woman of the same age. Montana and Idaho had 8 men over 21 for every woman; Nevada 5; Arizona 4; Washington 2.6; and Colorado 2.3. In order to attract more women and increase their populations and thereby better qualify for statehood, Wyoming and some of these other states jumped on the suffragettes' bandwagon.

In the Beginning

Full appreciation of the women's suffrage debate in the first Wyoming Territorial Legislature can only spring from an understanding of territorial governance. The United States Congress and the president needed to act to create a territory, name it, and then later, if qualified, create a state. Following its deliberative tradition, the United States Senate spent much time discussing the names for what would become Wyoming Territory. Some thought that Indian tribe names such as, Cheyenne, Shoshone, or Arapaho might strike a spark of interest, but others thought that the names of rivers including the Platte, the Big Horn, and Sweetwater might flow better.

At the end of the day, Lincoln and Wyoming became the two favorites. Wyoming had already been used as a place name in northeastern Pennsylvania, and derived from the Delaware Indians, who—surprise, surprise—settled along the Delaware River including areas of Pennsylvania. However, their real tribal name was the Lenape, and since they often served to settle disputes among rival tribes, they were sometimes called the "Grandfather" tribe. Eventually, like most Indians, the Delaware were forced from their homelands and pushed first to Ohio and then finally to Oklahoma, then known as Indian Territory.

During the final debate on the name of the new territory and its organization, Wyoming histories just barely mention John M. Ashley, a member of the U.S. House of Representatives and the early champion of Wyoming's territorial organization, who had suggested the name, Wyoming, as early as 1865. In fact, he was John Miller Ashley, a Republican member of the House, from Toledo, Ohio.

Ashley was born near Pittsburgh, Pennsylvania, on November 14, 1824. First as a clerk on river boats and then as a newspaper man, he certainly understood the history and waterways of the Delaware and Ohio Rivers, and his knowledge of the Delaware Indians and their language was based on his own geographic proximity to the tribe and his curiosity.

Ashley moved to Toledo in the late 1840s and worked in the wholesale drug business. In an odd twist of fate, Ashley moved to Toledo about the same time the Lenape or Delaware Indians were pushed from Pennsylvania and Delaware into Ohio.

After several more years, Ashley ran for Congress and served from March 4, 1859, to March 3, 1869. During his congressional service, he chaired the Committee on Territories, and that assignment was pivotal for Wyoming's future and its name. He worked on behalf of the fledgling territory and gave it the name that was drawn from the Indians.

At the end of his last term, Ashley changed course by 180 degrees and opposed Wyoming's territorial standing. He simply did not expect that any meaningful number of people would settle in Wyoming Territory. Perhaps his change of heart stemmed from the fact that in 1870, Ashley was appointed governor of Montana Territory, which then had no better settlement prospects than Wyoming.

After another successful career in the railroad business, he died on September 16, 1896, and his heirs began an Ohio political legacy that spanned several generations.

Although the residents of Wyoming were never consulted, when the elected officials in Washington, D.C., learned that the Delaware Indian word meant "at the big plains" or "on the great plains" the name fit the new territory like a pair of Levi jeans. The simplicity of the word and the ease of spelling also helped persuade the Senate to finally convey the name, Wyoming, to the new territory.

Like the "organic" acts of other territories,

Wyoming's founding territorial statute was drawn from the Ordinance of 1787, commonly known as the Northwest Ordinance. That ordinance provided the governmental organization for Ohio country and set the pattern for the organization of territories west of the Mississippi.

The purpose of the whole territorial system was to elevate western "colonies" or territories into states that would enjoy absolute parity with the original thirteen states. This arrangement was designed to avoid the colonial status of those original thirteen states which was imposed by England and led to the American Revolution. At the Ordinance's inception, a territory needed to reach a population of 60,000 to qualify for statehood.

The Organic Act of Wyoming, enacted by the fortieth Congress on July 25, 1868, gave the state a very simple territorial government. Or at least a functional one designed to serve a very, very small population until Wyoming might qualify for statehood.

Aside from establishing its boundaries, the organic acts gave the president of the United States the power to appoint the governor for a four year term with the consent of the U.S. Senate. In the same vein, the president had the power to appoint a secretary who would be the second in command. Legislative power was given to a council or "senate" of nine members and a house of representatives of thirteen members. The highest court in the territory was composed of three federal judges, also appointed by the president with the consent of the U.S. Senate. The

Saving the Best of the West in Wyoming

last office created by the act was the delegate to the U.S. House of Representatives who could discuss chamber matters, but could not vote. Of course, today only the District of Columbia's sole representative cannot vote.

Then President Andrew Johnson, an old fashioned southern Jacksonian Democrat who was vice president when Lincoln was assassinated, submitted several candidates for Wyoming's Territorial governor and secretary. The U.S. Senate, which was overwhelmingly Republican, took no action. The Radical Republicans in Congress, who saw Johnson favoring the old Confederacy during his Reconstruction program, became bitter enemies of the president and opposed him at every turn, including territorial appointments.

Again in another odd-ball twist, Wyoming, then an overwhelmingly Democratic state, applauded the Republican Senate's decision. After Ulysses S. Grant's election as president in 1868, and before his March 4, 1869 inauguration, he promised quick action on Wyoming's territorial appointments. Good to his word, President Grant appointed: John A. Campbell of Ohio, governor; Edward M. Lee of Connecticut, secretary; Joseph M. Carey of Pennsylvania, United States attorney; John H. Howe of Illinois, chief justice; William T. Jones of Indiana and John W. Kingman of New Hampshire, associate justices; and Church Howe of Massachusetts, U.S marshal. Supporting a Republican President and Civil War hero, the U.S. Senate quickly confirmed these Wyoming territorial appointments. All were Republicans, and many served just a short time.

Later that year, Stephen F. Nuckolls, a Democrat and prosperous Cheyenne merchant, ran—and won decisively—the non-voting delegate seat to the U.S. House of Representatives.

Arriving in Cheyenne by train in mid-May, 1869, the new officers eagerly took up their duties and began forming the new territorial government. Both Campbell, thirty-three years old, and Lee, thirty-one, were bachelors when they arrived in Wyoming. The two shared competence, enthusiasm for the tasks at hand, and a friendly working relationship. Both had served in the Union Army and risen to rank of brigadier general in the Civil War.

Campbell was born in Salem, Ohio, in 1835. When the Civil War broke out he was an editorial writer for the *Cleveland Leader*. He counted as his friends, President Grant and General Sheridan. He served as Assistant Secretary of War until Grant appointed him Wyoming's first territorial governor.

Campbell was a man of "position and fine tastes." He married in 1872, and served six years as territorial governor. In 1875, he was appointed third secretary of state and later, in ill health, served as the American counsel in Basel, Switzerland. He died in Washington D.C., on July 14, 1880.

Edward Lee was born in Guildford (more likely Guilford), Connecticut, in 1835. After law school he practiced in Detroit, Michigan. Later Lee practiced law and served in the Connecticut Legislature from 1866-1867.

Lee was also a gifted speaker. He served as

territorial secretary for just a single year. He was one of the founders of the *Wyoming Tribune* that later became the *Wyoming State Tribune*. He spent the last thirty years of his life in private law practice in New York. Lee died there on January 1, 1913.

After Wyoming's territorial Republican and Democratic conventions, the selection of candidates, and the general election on September 2, 1869, Secretary Lee called the two houses to order on October 12, 1869. When they convened, all nine members of the Council (upper chamber) and all thirteen members of the House of Representatives were Democrats. However, five members of the House were absent for the opening session or beyond. Eventually, all showed up, but one other member, J.M. Freeman, from the unorganized territory of far western Wyoming, never appeared.

William Bright of South Pass City was elected president of the Council and S.M. Curran of Carbon County was chosen as speaker of the House. While Wyoming's Organic Act permitted sixty day sessions, the Council met fifty days and the House met fifty-one.

Since no capitol buildings were even planned then, two rooms were rented in buildings about a block and a half apart. The Council met in the Thomas Leland Building and the House met in the Arcade Building.

The critical ingredients of early success were the drinks available at Luke Murrin's wholesale liquor house. His private sampling room provided the ideal gathering place for legislators who were well versed in the art of social drinking. Soon Luke's popularity led him to run and win election as the second mayor of Cheyenne. He was also an Irish immigrant.

By the standards of other inexperienced territorial legislatures or the corruption of its territorial officials, Wyoming's first session claimed itself hardworking and productive. However, when the two houses began their work, it did not appear that women's suffrage was much more than a passing thought. For example, the 1869 legislators tentatively approved Cheyenne as the state capitol; they selected Laramie as the site for the future penitentiary; they raised the pay of federal judges and their own; they legalized property taxes already levied prior to 1869, and provided for additional mill levies; they gave new protections to miners and railroad workers including the right of an injured railroad employee to sue the company for damages; they created Uinta County out of the previously unorganized western territory; they changed the boundaries of the four other counties; and then changed the name of Carter County to Sweetwater; they voted to override the governor's veto and thereby officially sanctioned and licensed gambling; and they overrode another veto of "an act to prevent intermarriage between white persons and those of Negro or Mongolian blood." At that moment, it did not appear that the legislators were imbued with the spirit of equality.

Saving the Best of the West in Wyoming

In the waning days of the first territorial legislature, through the leadership of a few, the members began to warm up to the idea of voting rights for women. Since four of the six individuals most associated with this debate and its subsequent impact lived in South Pass City, a brief detour to it in 1869 can help us understand this unusual fact.

Esther Hobart Morris, the territory and country's first woman justice of the peace, lived in South Pass City. John Kingman, Associate Supreme Justice and advocate for women's suffrage, who helped appoint Esther Morris, also called South Pass City home. The other two residents of South Pass City who were active in the suffrage debate included William Bright, president of the Territorial Council and also a supporter of women's right to vote, and one of his most vigorous opponents in that debate, Ben Sheets.

South Pass City

Although South Pass became the Oregon Trail's gateway to the West, South Pass City sprang up around 1867 when a group of miners bankrolled by Noyes Baldwin, then a Lander, Wyoming resident, established one of the first gold mining districts. Baldwin was no newcomer to the lodes of gold in South Pass City. After serving at Fort Douglas in Utah, in 1865, he was reassigned to Fort Bridger in southwestern Wyoming. Major Baldwin, commander of the Fort, led a group of soldiers who, while scouting the area, panned for gold in South Pass streams.

After leaving military service in 1866, Baldwin secured a license to trade with the Shoshone Indians and promoted gold mining as a means to attract more settlers to the area around South Pass and Lander. Later he became an early and revered Lander settler where he launched a successful Lander trading post.

Baldwin's investment in South Pass City's first "major" mining district was followed by few richer ones. With gold news reaching eastern Wyoming and Salt Lake City, the rush was on.

South Pass City was located along Willow Creek and seven miles north of the Oregon Trail. At its peak, the population reached near 2,000, and some estimated its peak at 3,000. Even at 2,000, that number exceeded the 1,450 of Cheyenne, then the largest city in Wyoming. As a result, for a short period it was even considered a competitor with Cheyenne for the site of the territorial capitol. It also served as the Carter County seat which later was renamed Sweetwater County. However, when the most productive mines went bust and the Union Pacific bypassed South Pass City, its decline was as rapid as its ascent.

By 1870, just 1,116 people lived in the mining area, and soon that dropped to under 500. By 1875, less than 100 people resided in South Pass City.

It is estimated that during its peak years from 1867 to 1873, only $2 million worth of gold was dug from its mines. By comparison, one of the early gold mines in southwestern Montana, Alder Gulch, produced $35 million worth of gold in just its first 5 years. In comparison to the other western gold mines, South Pass City, one of Wyoming's richest gold mines, was a minor mining camp and consequently mining never replaced the stock growers' frontier as the engine of early economic growth.

South Pass City's major role in the early days of territorial government and the suffrage debate appears to be a function of its earlier status as a major city in the larger Carter County and an outdated impression that the city was robust and influential. In those days, news did not travel fast. Briefly, as one of the few larger towns in southwest Wyoming, it may also have offered a pool of talent that could politically balance the eastern part of the state.

The Suffrage Legislation

William Bright, the first elected president of the Council or upper chamber, introduced the suffrage bill on the forty-second day of the fifty day legislative session. After a stint as a miner, Bright, who was then forty-five years old, chose one of Wyoming's leading professions, the job of saloonkeeper in South Pass City. He had just moved there with his wife a year earlier in 1868.

As a native of Virginia, he had served as a major in the Quartermaster Corps in Washington, D.C. In 1867, he and his wife, who was twenty years his junior, moved to Salt Lake City where he worked as a postal inspector until they joined a small gold rush to South Pass City. Like many others in South Pass City, Bright's path to riches took a long detour. The county tax records revealed that his saloon, cabin, and personal property were valued at $658. In today's inflation adjusted terms, his net worth would stand near $16,000.

Although for some reason known as "Colonel" instead of "Major" Bright, he had never attended school and could not remember where or when he had learned to read. Bright was not a learned man, and certainly did not follow the East Coast suffragettes, their lectures, or newspapers.

His calculus was disarmingly straightforward. Since he believed that his wife, Julia, and his mother had just as much right to the franchise as the Negroes who had just received it, he introduced the bill, Council Bill No. 70, and managed it. He also adored his young wife, and she was reported to have been firmly committed to women's suffrage. Later, they would move to Denver, Colorado, where they played minor roles in Colorado's suffrage campaign of 1876-1877.

Working diligently with Bright on this legislation was Edward Lee, the Secretary of Wyoming Territory. He was the only true suffragist featured in the legislative debate over women's right to vote. His earlier legislative experience in Connecticut, including his introduction of an unsuccessful women's suffrage bill, his speaking ability, and his sound working relationship with the Wyoming legislators made him a powerful ally.

Since in the 1860s, Wyoming women did not speak in public and had no suffrage organization, Lee became the public face and advocate for women's voting rights.

Saving the Best of the West in Wyoming

At that time these two "new immigrants" and others like them may have been the "best and brightest" of the Wyoming frontier. This immigrant tradition would prove to be one of the few catalysts of change and innovation throughout Wyoming history.

Although simple justice seemed to motivate Bright and Lee, they knew that the suffrage bill could only be sold to the legislators as a means to attract more women to the territory and increase its population and thus the prospects for statehood. The Council passed the bill 6 to 2 (one member was absent), but it met stiff resistance in the House where another South Pass City resident and young bachelor lawyer, Ben Sheets, led the opposition.

The press did not cover the debate and the official record is sparse, but it is known that first Sheets and others tried to adjourn the House so the bill would die. Failing to adjourn, Sheets and his allies did try "killer" amendments to derail the bill. For example, for the word, "women," he tried to insert "all colored women and squaws." At the end of the day, the presumed marketing appeal of the bill and the hope that Governor Campbell might veto it produced a House vote seven to four in favor.

The governor had not yet made up his mind on the matter. After four days of uncertainty during which all three territorial Supreme Court justices encouraged him to sign it, Campbell did so.

The wildness, the near ungovernable nature of the Wyoming frontier, and the racial and gender hostility of the state and its first territorial legislature suggest that the most persuasive argument for women's rights was its public relations value.

In a similar concession to reality and after the bill became law, many participants and observers stated that the entire process had been a joke. For example and as cited in T.A. Larson's *History of Wyoming*, in an October 8, 1870, editorial in the *Wyoming Tribune,* Secretary Lee wrote, "...How strange that a movement destined to purify the muddy pool of politics... should have originated as a joke... All honor to them, say we, to Wyoming's first legislature!"

Joking aside, fearing women's growing preference for the Republican Party (still the party of Lincoln), the solid Democratic majorities in the 1871 legislature vowed to repeal the measure and override the governor's veto. Unconvinced by any appeal for equality, the Democrats voted to repeal the suffrage law. As expected, Governor Campbell vetoed the repeal, but surprisingly the Council failed to override by a single vote.

After the near extinction of voting rights for Wyoming women in 1871, those rights became main stream elements of territorial life. But as we will see, obstacles to the practice of those rights persisted for years.

The story of women's suffrage would not be complete without the tale of Esther Hobart Morris, who served briefly as Wyoming's and the country's first female justice of the peace. Section 9 of the

Saving the Best of the West in Wyoming

Organic Act of Wyoming stated that "justices of the peace shall have no jurisdiction over any matter in controversy when the title or boundaries of land may be in dispute, or where the debt or sum claimed shall exceed one hundred dollars...." As in other territories, all other matters of law were given to the supreme and district courts.

Edward Lee, the territorial secretary, became acting governor whenever Governor Campbell traveled outside of the Territory. On February 14, 1870, when Campbell visited the East, Lee, with the help of John Kingman, a territorial associate Supreme Court justice and another advocate for women's suffrage, appointed three women to fill justice of the peace vacancies.

As it turned out, only Esther Morris was duly qualified and served. She replaced a man who had resigned. The two other women given that same commission were Mrs. Caroline Neil from Rocks Point, Wyoming, and Mrs. Francis Gallagher from South Pass City. It is not clear if either one actually served or where they might have been assigned.

In 1814, Esther Hobart Morris was born near Spencer, New York, and her father's name was Daniel McQuigg. Her middle name, Hobart, was her mother's maiden name. After the death of her parents, she worked as milliner and at the age of twenty-eight married Artemus Slack, a civil engineer, who died soon after the birth of their son, Archibald. Esther moved to Peru, Illinois, where she met and married John Morris, a Polish immigrant. They had twin sons.

When appointed justice of the peace, Esther was still married to John Morris. Like William Bright, John Morris was a saloonkeeper and miner, but less successful. John Morris and his step-son, Archibald, arrived in South Pass City in 1868, the same year as the Bright family. In July, 1869, Esther Morris and the twins joined them.

At the time of her appointment, Esther Morris was fifty-seven years old. She stood six feet tall and weighed 180 pounds. She was mannish in appearance and blunt in conversation. Her formal education had ended when she was orphaned at the age of fourteen. She possessed no meaningful speaking or writing skills. Her justice of the peace duties encompassed the 460 people then living in South Pass City. She was no activist nor a forerunner of the suffragettes. She advised women to have confidence in the good will of men and not to pester them.

Her term lasted only eight and a half months and ended in November, 1870. She handled a total of 26 cases or one case every 10 days. Twelve were criminal cases and 14 were civil cases, and most of them were assault and battery cases and small debt collections.

Her eighteen year old son, Robert, was her clerk, and her total fees were $135.70 or $5.22 per case. She wished to continue, but no political party would nominate her, so she could not run for election.

In June, 1871, seven months after she left office, Esther Morris swore out a warrant for her husband's arrest on the grounds of assault and battery, but that case was settled out of court. She left him in 1873 and moved to Albany, New York. Later she moved to Springfield, Illinois, and in the 1880s Esther moved back to Wyoming and lived with her son, Robert, in Cheyenne. She died in 1902.

John Morris was elected Sweetwater County (formerly Carter County) coroner in 1872, and in 1877, he died in South Pass City.

William Bright, Edward Lee, and Governor John Campbell were the true champions of women's suffrage in Wyoming Territory. Only a very creative history allowed Esther Morris to eclipse them.

Other female elected officials were much more accomplished than Esther Morris. For example, in 1894 Estelle Reel was elected State Superintendent of Public Instruction and was the first woman in the U.S. elected to a statewide office. In 1898, Reel was also appointed National Superintendent of Indian Schools by President McKinley and was the first woman presidential appointee confirmed by the U.S. Senate.

Giving new impetus to this misleading history, in 1955, Esther Morris was chosen as Wyoming's outstanding deceased citizen and had her statue placed in the U.S. Capitol's Statuary Hall and in front of the state capital in Cheyenne. While she did serve as Wyoming and the country's first woman justice of the peace at a time when women had few practical rights, the myth of Esther Morris stands in perfect symmetry with the broader myth of Wyoming as the Equality State.

Wyoming history is also dotted with real heroes and heroines such as frontiersmen and explorer, John Colter; Shoshone warrior and chief, Washakie; preeminent psychologist, philosopher, educator, and poet, June Etta Downey; Mary Garrett, the first woman in the United States elected justice of the peace in 1902 and who served twenty years in that elected judicial position; and more recently songwriter, singer, bronze sculptor, and rodeo champion, Chris LeDoux.

Making myths of the Equality State and Esther Morris even more indigestible is the fact that no one woman can represent the history of women in Wyoming. Too many women played decisive roles in the settlement and growth of the state. They ranged from ranch women to school teachers and writers.

A few of these women, who are not household names, but who contributed so much to Wyoming's settlement and culture, can illustrate the richness and breadth of this role.

Verla Ritchie Sommers, a Sublette County cowgirl and ranch woman, started gathering cattle and desert horses for her dad when she was twelve years old. She started haying with horses when she was thirteen. In an interview with Carol Rankin well before her death she said, "It took us about forty-five days to do all of the haying, so we'd have to use two teams of horses a day. I'd harness one team in the morning and then at noon I'd change teams. This kept the horses fresh so they wouldn't play out on us before the haying season was over. I never drove a tractor until I was married.

A young woman, Helen Coburn, and a family friend, Mary Culbertson, left their Carroll, Iowa, homes and traveling by train and stage coach, finally arrived in Worland, Wyoming, in September, 1905. Aside from a rifle and pistol, Helen brought her golf clubs, tennis racket, and umbrella. Worland was a small frontier town with just a few buildings and a small log hotel. A golf course and tennis courts were far in the future.

While their fathers and families would later move to Worland and build irrigation canals, the two single women took up adjoining homesteads about eighteen miles from town. Not only did they help battle a typhoid fever epidemic just after they arrived, but each proved up on her homestead in 1907. When the teacher selected for the thirty pupil Worland school district chose not to serve, Helen agreed to serve as the temporary teacher. She rode horseback and crossed a river every day to teach.

In 1908, she married Ashby Howell, the owner of the Worland general store. They lived in town and both became decisive forces in the growth of Worland. Whether due to a young age, death, abandonment, spousal abuse or divorce, Helen and Mary represented many single women homesteaders who beat the odds and helped foster the development of Wyoming and its civic culture.

A similar but perhaps more remarkable story is the life of Geraldine Lucas, who after an early and unsuccessful marriage, raised her son alone and even returned to school at Oberlin College. After a teaching career in New York City and at the age of forty-seven, she left New York and homesteaded at the foot of the Grand Teton near Jackson Hole, Wyoming.

In 1924, when she was fifty-nine, she joined five other climbers and scaled the Grand Teton. She was the second woman to accomplish that feat.

Perhaps trying to make amends for the early historians, who mythologized Esther Morris, the American Heritage Center at the University of Wyoming nominated Caroline Cameron Lockhart as Wyoming Citizen of the Century. She was an extraordinary, but almost unknown woman, who comes close to capturing the stereotype of the Western heroine.

She was born on the family farm in Eagle Pointe, Illinois, on February 24, 1871. After college and unable to establish herself as an actress, at age eighteen she debuted as a reporter for *The Boston Post.* By reporting on everything from "taking the wheel of a double-rigged ship" to spending Christmas Eve in a poor Boston neighborhood, she broke the mold for woman reporters of that day.

In 1895, she interviewed Buffalo Bill Cody when the Wild West Show was in Boston. Cody later joined Caroline Lockhart as another nominee for Wyoming Citizen of the Century.

Saving the Best of the West in Wyoming

Lockhart began writing short stories, and in 1900 she accepted a position as columnist for the *Philadelphia Bulletin.* She wrote the column under the pseudonym, Suzette. Assigned by her paper in 1904 to write a feature on the Blackfeet Indians, she traveled to Cody. Except for travel and work in Denver for the *Post,* she lived in the Cody area for the rest of her life.

From 1904-1915, Lockhart concentrated on writing, and while continuing to sell newspaper articles and a few short stories, she finished her first western novel, *Me-Smith,* which brought her national recognition. By 1915, Lockhart had written three more novels and her novel, *The Man from Bitter Roots,* was made into a Hollywood movie.

She wrote four more novels including an exaggerated tale based on the life of Wyoming sheepherder Lucy Morrison Moore, also known as the "Sheep Queen of Wyoming." Her novel and the subsequent movie, *The Fighting Shepherdess,* was her most popular since *Me-Smith.* Although Moore did work sheep and live in a sheep wagon, later she lived in a comfortable home in Casper during the winter, was well-to-do, enjoyed the good life, and speculated in Los Angeles real estate.

In 1920, Lockhart was a founder and then first president of the Cody Stampede, the now famous summertime rodeo in western Wyoming. She was an accomplished horsewoman, and her opposition to Prohibition, her affairs with men, and her outspoken nature clashed with the more conservative members of Cody society.

From 1920 to 1925, Lockhart owned the *Park*

County Enterprise, which was renamed the *Cody Enterprise* in 1921. In 1926, after consolidating the *Cody Enterprise* with another newspaper, she fulfilled a dream and bought a ranch, the L Slash Heart, in Dryhead, Montana. She grew the ranch from one hundred sixty acres to 6,034 acres. In 1935, her steers topped the Omaha cattle market.

She still spent her winters in Cody, and in 1933, she wrote her last book, *The Old and New West*. In 1952 and in her eighties, she moved back to Cody full-time. Later she sold her Montana ranch.

Throughout her life she was involved with many men, but never married. Even at age eighty-eight, Lockhart found a much younger boyfriend who was in his sixties. She set the early standard for the western novel and the Hollywood westerns of John Ford and John Wayne. She lived an independent and remarkably productive life and set an example for many women who would follow. She died in 1962, at the age of ninety-one.

While these women better represent the role of women in Wyoming history, let's look at what happened to Wyoming women just after the suffrage legislation passed and after Esther Morris served her eight and a half months as South Pass City's justice of the peace.

The suffrage bill immediately gave one thousand voting age women the franchise to vote and run for elected office, and they had their first chance to exercise those rights in the 1870 election. But the secret ballot was not introduced in Wyoming until 1890, and in that same year the ratio of voting age men to voting age women still stood at three to one.

To assess the public relations value of Wyoming's legislation and according to T.A. Larson's *History of Wyoming*, we need only consult W.F. Poole's thoroughly researched *Index to Periodical Literature*. Covering the period before 1869 through 1881, under the heading "Wyoming" only a total of six articles were listed. Two discussed the territory generally, two its botany, and two its geology. Not one mentioned women's suffrage.

In 1870-1871, the women in Cheyenne and Laramie were summoned to serve and did serve on grand and petit juries. However, new judges in those cities decreed that jury duty was not a necessary adjunct of suffrage. It was not until 1950, when Wyoming women were summoned again and able to serve on juries.

Counting from the early 1870s over a twenty year span, only two women ran for the territorial and later the state legislature. According to T.A. Larson's history, when at least 500 votes were required to win, one candidate received 8 votes and the other tallied 5.

Wyoming did not elect a woman to the state legislature until 1910—forty years after they were afforded the right to run for elected office. That woman was Mary or "Mollie" Bellamy, a school teacher who later became the Albany County Superintendent of Public Schools. By comparison, Colorado, the second state to award women the right to vote, gave women that franchise by referendum in 1893. Just over 65,000 registered voters participated in that election, and 55% supported women's voting rights. One year later on November 6, 1894, Colorado elected the first three women in the nation to its state legislature.

Although three women were nominated, not one was elected to Wyoming's constitutional convention in 1889.

Again as written by T.A. Larson in his classic history of Wyoming, Hubert Howe Bancroft, who catalogued several western state histories, sent his researchers to Wyoming in 1885. They interviewed more than one hundred leading citizens. Not one was a woman, and no mention was made of Esther Morris.

Let's fast forward and see how women have faired in the Wyoming legislature. Today, in the 30 member Senate, 4 women senators have been elected and serve. They represent 13% of that chamber. In the 60 member House 17 members are women or 28% of the House. Between 1910 and 2004—a period of 94 years—a total of 79 women were elected to Wyoming's House.

In comparison to the number of women in other state legislatures, 39 legislatures have more women than Wyoming. Wyoming's 21 women members tie it with Louisiana, and 9 legislatures have fewer than 21 women members.

Of the total of 1,739 women legislators now serving throughout the nation—nearly 24% of all legislators—1,194 are Democrats and 535 are Republicans.

Saving the Best of the West in Wyoming

The gap between the symbols of the Equality State and its performance has now persisted for almost 140 years. Other symbols such as the "first woman governor," Nellie Tayloe Ross, and the 1920s "petticoat government" of Jackson Hole, Wyoming, (one of the first all women's town councils in the United States), cannot erase this record.

Admittedly, the Wyoming Territory and its frontier were inhospitable to women. It was often said that in its early days Wyoming was "hell on women and horses." However, after more than a century of visible inequality between men and women, Wyoming's leaders and their spouses might have taken some real corrective action beyond placing Esther Morris' statue in the U.S. Capitol and celebrating the nation's first woman governor.

Nellie Tayloe Ross was indeed overwhelmingly elected on November 4, 1824, to finish the two remaining years of her husband's first term.

Mrs. Miriam Amanda or "Ma" Ferguson was elected governor of Texas on the same day as Nellie, but Nellie was inaugurated twenty days before Mrs. Ferguson. That is the basis for the claim that Nellie Tayloe Ross was the first woman governor. However, they shared another claim to "fame." They both succeeded their husbands as governor.

Nellie's husband, William B. Ross, died in office, but Ma's husband, James Edward Ferguson, was impeached and ineligible for re-election.

In 1926, the Democratic Party nominated Nellie again as its candidate for governor, but she lost, and never again ran for public office in Wyoming. She moved to Washington, D.C., and worked as director of the Democratic National Committee's Women's Division and later was appointed the first woman director of the Mint. She served in that position from 1933-1953. She retired in Washington, D.C., and died at the age of 101 on December 19, 1977.

New Departures

The primary purpose of this chapter has been to shine the "Light of Knowledge" on the myth of the Equality State, but a blueprint of ideas can improve the lot of Wyoming women.

Historically, when the stock growers dominated the Wyoming economy—or at least competed with mining as the leading industry—ranching, for most men and women, was not a lucrative profession. Even today, the average annual income for ranchers is $30,790. However, since those earlier days, the state's occupational structure and wages have changed dramatically.

The Bureau of Labor Statistics 2007 and most recent Occupational Employment and Wage Estimates for Wyoming provide a unique look at the economic condition and opportunities for Wyoming's working women. In future years the absolute value of these wage estimates may change, but the relative earning power of the different occupations will no doubt remain fairly constant. Today's high wage occupations will also be tomorrow's best paying jobs, and today's low wage jobs will remain near the bottom of tomorrow's wage scale.

This data and research yields three measures that can benefit Wyoming women. But first let's set the stage.

Wyoming has witnessed a decade long economic expansion that has seen extraordinary employment growth and a very sizable drop in the unemployment rate. For example, since November, 2005, the statewide unemployment rate has been well under 4%. Between 2001 and 2008, Wyoming has witnessed job growth of almost thirty percent. From 1990 to 2008, per capita personal income grew from $18,000 to just over $47,000—a growth rate of just over 160%.

While the unemployment numbers will fluctuate from month to month and year to year, during the next few years, Wyoming's economy will perform better than the national economy and most state economies, particularly when measured by per capita personal income.

In the near-term it appears that Wyoming's unemployment rate will hover at a little less than half of the nation's unemployment rate. Regional growth hubs such as Albany, Campbell, and Sublette counties provide even greater economic opportunity.

Saving the Best of the West in Wyoming

When the national unemployment rate rises, eventually so will Wyoming's unemployment rate. While Wyoming's unemployment rate lags the national rate, if the U.S. economy has a bout of pneumonia, Wyoming's economy will just catch a cold—at least until the energy industry begins to exhaust its reserves.

Over time, the demand for workers has far outstripped the supply, and that demand will return. Under these circumstances, improving the earning power and upward mobility of women should have been a "cake walk," particularly in view of the state revenue generated by this longer-term growth. Much of this recent growth can be attributed to the natural resource and mining industry, government, wholesale trade, education, and health services.

In the short-run, the 2008-2009 recession and financial crisis may prompt a slow down in Wyoming's economic growth rate, but the medium-term looks just as bright as the recent past. Later, we will see that the traditional sources of growth will eventually decline, but they will allow a transition to a more diverse and sustainable economy.

The second important economic fact to keep in mind is that Wyoming's full-time employees (273,170) earn an average hourly rate of $17.36 and an average annual income of $36,100.

The first big step towards improving the economic lot of Wyoming women means that whatever the job or occupation, they should be paid the same amount as men—equal pay for equal work—not a new or radical principle.

Wyoming women have been over-represented in professions that, on average, pay less than others. Some of those are: *community and social services,* including social workers and counselors*; healthcare support* that encompasses nurse aides, dental assistants, and veterinary assistant*s;* and *food preparation and serving.*

For example, those in the food preparation business earn a yearly average of $17,880—less than one half of the state average. Healthcare support personnel on average make $24,310 a year. Community and social service occupations average $34,380 a year,

In these lower paying but critical service professions women should have more opportunity for training, education, and advancement.

Reaching the goal of pay equity will require a change in attitude among male managers, active recruitment, education, and on-the-job training for women. State government or private companies can offer women educational benefits, such as the repayment of student loans and scholarships. The employers in these fields must take responsibility for these initiatives, and this investment should produce excellent returns. Elected officials, including school boards, need to assume their fair share of this investment. Beyond ending decades of inequality, it's the smart thing to do.

Secondly, women need to have better access to the highest paying jobs. Wyoming needs to break the "glass ceiling" for its better educated and experienced women. Of course, that means hiring more women in management jobs and promoting them to chief financial officer and chief executive positions.

Women should also be given much better opportunities for higher paying, non-traditional jobs in fields such as *architecture and engineering, oil and gas, and the life, physical, and social science occupations.*

For example, the annual average salary for architects and engineers is $59,300, with chemical engineers making $75,350. In the physical sciences, biologists can earn an average of $57,530, and hydrologists can make $54,440.

The third prescription holds that the best and widest range of employment opportunities can only come from a concerted effort to diversify Wyoming's natural resource dependent economy. Otherwise, the base of very good jobs will remain small, and many women will continue to be limited to the lower paying sectors, such as food service, personal care, and health care support.

Since energy prices will inevitably rebound, the energy industry will grow again, and that growth can give Wyoming the breathing room to diversify. Wind energy, clean coal technology, carbon sequestration, and new energy pipelines can help to transition and sustain a new economy.

The construction of a more sustainable and equitable economy just takes imagination and a willingness to experiment. Other states have embraced innovation and met success. For example, Nebraska's Advantage program attracts businesses with high paying jobs. Eligible companies, that at a minimum must create at least 75 new and high wage jobs, are given a 15% investment tax credit and a 10% wage credit. The program is on its way to creating 12,000 new high-wage jobs. The Accelerate Wisconsin initiative offers $5 million every year in grants or loans for start-up companies and new business incubators. Wisconsin has also expanded its venture capital tax credit that will reach $100 million in 2015. That alone has increased venture capital investment by $44 million.

In a strategy to recruit and retain workers less than thirty-five years old, Iowa is planning to offer a student loan repayment program for those who live in Iowa and work in "critical needs professions" such as nursing. The Hawkeye State may create a full tuition and merit-based scholarship program for its best students who commit to live in Iowa for a certain period of time.

Florida, Indiana, Kentucky, Maine, Missouri, Texas, and Washington have all created something akin to "innovation and commerce centers" that are either co-located with the state's community colleges, universities, or vital growth industries. Each has an "enterprise fund" that can give seed money to start-up companies, rural development projects, and new or current businesses that need additional financing to expand.

These programs and many others show that Wyoming's path to a diverse and growing economy is as long or short as its imagination and political will. By virtue of its $2.5 billion in annual tourism revenue, which drives a host of well paying professions including marketing, computer science, art sales, and real estate,

Saving the Best of the West in Wyoming

Wyoming could jump start this strategy to diversify. As we pursue this course, we can only hope that history will not be our guide.

Equality Day and More

In the last century, four demographic features of Wyoming have stood in sharp relief—first, the very small number of residents; second, the extremely low population density; third, the scarcity of women; and fourth, the blinding whiteness of the state's population.

Fortunately, the percentage of women living in Wyoming has now grown to 49.7% of the total population compared to the 50.8% of the U.S. population. However, the 2006 American Community Survey reveals that 91.8% of the population, including both men and women, is exclusively white. That compares to 73.9% of the U.S. population.

Saving the Best of the West in Wyoming

Other salient facts are:

1) Blacks or African Americans in Wyoming number 0.7% of the population compared to 12.4% for the U.S. The number of Wyoming blacks is so small that no statistically reliable sample can show other demographic characteristics such as poverty rates or education.

2) Hispanics or Latinos in Wyoming represent 6.9% of the population compared to 14.8% in the United States. Of the 35,732 Hispanics or Latinos living in Wyoming, 11.7% live in poverty.

3) Asian Americans living in Wyoming constitute 0.9% compared to 4.4% nationwide, and again their numbers are so small no other demographic lines can be drawn.

4) When it comes to American Indians, Wyoming can assert some supremacy. They comprise 2.2% of Wyoming's population compared to a mere .8% for the U.S. as a whole. However, 30.4% of our Indians live in poverty compared to the 26.6% of the U.S. Indian population.

Similar to Wyoming's long standing inequality between men and women, the condition of other minorities has not changed much in the last one hundred years, either. For example, the 1880 Census shows that of the 700 cowboys in Wyoming, 9 were Indians and 2 were black.

Another similar small black speck in Wyoming's very white territorial social landscape, was William Jefferson Hardin, the first and only black to serve in the territorial legislature. He served as member of the House from 1879 to 1882. He has been the forgotten man of Wyoming territorial and state history that so crowed about equal rights.

Hardin was born in Russellville, Kentucky, in 1831. His mother was one-fourth black and his father white. He was educated by Shakers and became a teacher. In 1863, he moved to Denver in Colorado Territory, because initially all men in the western territories over twenty-one had the right to vote. That changed in 1864 when blacks were temporarily excluded from voting.

Hardin was a stirring speaker and effective advocate for the repeal of the law denying blacks voting rights. In 1867, the U.S. Congress voted to restore those rights. Hardin was also a powerful spokesman for public education for black children.

Not surprisingly, Hardin was a member of the party of Lincoln. He became an at-large delegate to the 1872 Republican National Convention. He then earned an appointment as a weigher at the Denver Mint.

His Colorado political and economic future darkened when, after marrying a white Denver woman in 1873, he was confronted by Caroline K. Hardin who appeared with documents that proved he was already married to her. He fled Denver for Cheyenne, Wyoming, and became a barber and legislator. It is thought that Hardin

Saving the Best of the West in Wyoming

died in Leadville, Colorado in 1889 or 1890.

Our trip through Wyoming's byways of inequality has just begun.

The Rock Springs Massacre

On September 2, 1885, and reflecting a deep seated racism against Chinese immigrant labor and a legitimate resentment against the Union Pacific Coal Department, about 150 white men in Rock Springs, Wyoming, armed with rifles, moved toward the living quarters of the Chinese. They killed 28, wounded 15 others, caused almost $150,000 in property damage, and chased the surviving Chinese out of town. This troublesome action became known as the Rock Springs Massacre.

For years the Union Pacific's coal mines at Rock Springs had employed exclusively white miners, and many were recent immigrants. In 1875, a strike broke out and the Union Pacific

Saving the Best of the West in Wyoming

brought in Chinese workers, giving them better work assignments but paying them less.

Few doubt that the Union Pacific used the Chinese miners to undercut the wages of the white miners and halt the disruptions and early organizing in the mines. At the time of the massacre, 150 whites and 331 Chinese worked in the Rock Springs mines. Most other white miners had been fired.

By the 1880s, a wave of around 100,000 Chinese had settled throughout the West. Among the many whites predisposed towards racism, it prompted "anti-coolie" sentiment and violence. In 1882, the U.S. Congress even passed the Chinese Exclusion Act which suspended Chinese immigration for ten years, but the Rock Springs Massacre reached the pinnacle of prejudice and violence.

After the massacre in 1885, Wyoming's Governor Warren requested federal troops, and they arrived to escort the Chinese back to the coal mines and maintain the peace. The troops established Camp Pilot Butte, which finally closed thirteen years later in 1898.

Citing the culpability of the Union Pacific, the grand jury issued no indictments against the white miners, and Wyoming refused to give the Chinese government any compensation for the loss of life and property. Eventually, and accepting no liability, the U.S. Congress approved the payment of property losses totaling $147,748.74.

Civil Rights

One other historical event can shine even more light on Wyoming's myth of equality.

In 1954, the Plains Hotel in Cheyenne, Wyoming, refused service to a black serviceman and his wife. That began a three year painful journey to the 1957 Wyoming Civil Rights Act that attempted to ensure equal access to hotels, restaurants, and other public accommodations.

In early 1957, 21 states had no public accommodation laws and 15 of those were in the South. Wyoming was one of only 6 non-southern states that did not guarantee equal access.

When the legislation was finally passed, the enforcement of the law was turned over to the counties and the fines were of little consequence.

Saving the Best of the West in Wyoming

Fortunately for the 2,557 African Americans living in Wyoming during the 1960s, the landmark 1964 Civil Rights Act preempted Wyoming's anemic law. It was also not until 1965 that Wyoming eliminated all legal obstacles to interracial marriage.

When a society and culture are so homogenous, rural, and treat their women—who are also mainly white—as second class citizens, intolerance and discrimination usually becomes imbedded in the culture. Undoubtedly, over the past century Wyoming has made some strides towards racial, ethnic and religious tolerance, but today, in the 21st Century, its unspoken prejudice has evolved into a growing danger.

Let's briefly highlight a few more cases that poignantly capture this prejudice.

In 1983, as a memorial to the slain civil rights leader, Martin Luther King, Jr., the Congress of the United States designated a national holiday in King's honor. It falls on the third Monday in January near King's January 15, birthday. The day is set aside as a day to observe his birth and contributions to justice. For the past nearly twenty-five years, that day has been treated just like other national holidays—government offices, schools and many businesses are closed, and events are scheduled to commerate Dr. King, *except in Wyoming.*

On March 15, 1990, after seven years of bitter debate, the Wyoming legislature—one of the last to take action—finally passed a bill that named the

holiday "Martin Luther King Jr./Equality Day."
Depending on where, within the state, someone
lives, they might celebrate Equality Day or Martin
Luther King Jr. Day.

Here, in Sublette County, we celebrate
"Equality Day" instead of Martin Luther
King, Jr.'s birthday, and schools (for teachers and
administrators) and businesses, remain open.

In the fall, Sublette County celebrates it own
special holiday, "Hunting Day," when schools
close. Hunting Day, celebrated in other states,
too, is an artifact of a time when elk season
in many hunting areas opened on the same day.
However, today the season opens on many
different days. Yet when choosing between
Equality Day or "Hunting Day," many school
districts in Wyoming close on hunting day—
even though fewer and fewer families hunt.

As an example, the 2007 Wyoming Game and
Fish Department's Annual Report shows that
between 2002 and 2006 the number of elk
licenses has declined from 62,013 to 57,682 or
by 4,331 licenses—a 10% decline despite a total
elk population of 102,281 that is 23% above its
preferred population.

The woman legislator who successfully
spearheaded the legislative charge that resulted
in the 1990 passage of the Wyoming bill honoring
Dr. King was Harriet Elizabeth Byrd, the first
Wyoming black legislator since statehood. She
was born in 1926, and her birth in Cheyenne
marked the fourth generation of the Rhone family

in Wyoming. Her grandfather, Charles J. Rhone, who arrived in Wyoming as a child in 1876, later became a well-known cowboy and worked on the railroad. His son and Liz Byrd's father, Buck Rhone, also worked as a machinist for the railroad.

After graduating from Cheyenne High School in 1944, Liz attended a predominately black college, West Virginia State, and sought a degree in education. Following graduation in 1949, she returned to Cheyenne to begin her teaching career.

Despite being a well-educated and fourth generation Wyomingite, due to the color of her skin, her home town school district refused to hire her. After ten years of teaching at the F.E. Warren Air Force Base in Cheyenne, she finally earned a job in the Laramie County School District. Ten years after that, she was finally recognized as Wyoming's Teacher of the Year.

Looking to improve the benefits for teachers, she ran as a Democrat for a state House seat. She won and served for eight years. Then in 1988, she ran for a state Senate seat in Laramie County and won that as well. Two years later, she led Wyoming to at least partially honor Martin Luther King and take one small step towards real equality.

The State of **EQUALITY** In the Equality State

Indians

Very few, if any states, over the years can claim a dramatic elevation in the economic and social welfare of the Indian tribes within their borders. With the grant of sovereignty, the tribes and their reservations posed and still pose a complex web of tribal, state, and federal relations and responsibilities. Some states work to enhance the self-sufficiency and self-respect of their tribes, and the legal right to gambling has been a financial and economic bonanza for many. But when it came time for Wyoming state officials to support and negotiate in good faith the Wind River Indian Reservation's compact that codified its legal right to gambling, the state said no.

That position shone another light on

Saving the Best of the West in Wyoming

Wyoming's culture of intolerance. In a territory and state that in the past so enthusiastically embraced gambling of all kinds for its white citizens, that opposition was a cruel irony.

We know that in 1869, the first Wyoming territorial legislature voted to legalize gambling which had become a favorite Wyoming pastime and passion. In 1901, the Wyoming legislature voted to prohibit gambling, but the law was rarely enforced. Then in 1935, recognizing reality, the legislature reversed course and voted to legalize gambling. Governor Leslie Miller vetoed the bill. Not surrendering, the legislature voted to legalize pari-mutuel betting (horse and dog racing). That bill was signed into law. Finally, in the 1970s, Wyoming approved "social gambling" for charities and nonprofits.

As Wyoming expanded its gambling franchise for its citizens, the rest of the country was wrestling with the rights of Indian tribes to that same franchise. First, in 1987, the U.S. Supreme Court prevented states from regulating gambling on Indian reservations. If a state allowed gambling, the same form of gambling must be allowed on the Indian reservations within that state's borders. In 1988, Congress approved the Indian Gaming Regulatory Act (IGRA) requiring states to negotiate in good faith with tribes over what types of gambling would be allowed on its Indian reservations.

In June, 1992, and in accordance with the new law, the Eastern Shoshone and Northern Arapaho began discussions with Wyoming state officials over the Wind River Reservation's gaming compact. Insisting that the state did not allow gambling, even including lotteries such as Powerball, for a decade—from November 1994, through July, 2004—Wyoming used every means available, including a ballot initiative, legislation, lawsuits, and legal appeals to prohibit Indian gaming.

Finally, in July, 2005, in a nine to three vote, the Federal Appeals Court upheld a lower court ruling in favor of the Northern Arapaho, and declared that the tribe was entitled to Las Vegas style casino gambling. The Northern Arapaho became the first tribe in the nation to receive federal approval for such gambling without a tribal-state compact.

After one more year of state shenanigans, the Eastern Shoshone prevailed and won a compact from the state allowing casino-style gambling. Both tribes have now built and operate successful casinos.

During Wyoming's decade-long intransigence with its tribes, 249 of 562 federally recognized tribes, entered into tribal-state compacts. Twenty-eight states sanctioned Tribal Governmental gaming. Those games have produced $25.7 billion in revenue; created almost 700,000 jobs; reduced cash transfers to Indians by 32%; and promoted self-reliance and economic development. What was Wyoming thinking?

Matthew Shepard

Even today, ten years after Matthew Shepard's murder, rereading and recounting it is still a bone chilling and profoundly disturbing experience. Matthew Shepard was a talented and caring twenty-one year old gay University of Wyoming student. In a savage hate crime, he was beaten, burned, tortured, and pistol whipped with a .357 magnum. Unconscious, his two assailants tied him, spread eagle, to a wooden fence outside of Laramie, Wyoming, where he hung for twelve hours in near freezing temperatures. Police records state that he begged for his life.

Matthew's skull was fractured so that his skull was compressed into his brain. When first discovered on the fence by a passerby, he was thought to be a scarecrow. Later he died on October 12, 1998.

His two assailants, Aaron McKinney and Russell Henderson, were convicted and each given two consecutive life sentences.

At the time of his death, 22 states and the District of Columbia had hate crime laws that included sexual orientation. Eighteen states had hate crime laws that did not include sexual orientation, and 8 had no hate crime laws at all, including Wyoming.

Little has changed on the legal front, including the failure to pass a national hate crime law named as a memorial to Matthew Shepard. However, the scale of the problem has changed for the worse. In 2006, the FBI reported 7,720 single bias incidents. Of those 51.8% were racially motivated; 18.9% resulted from religious bias; 15.5% were motivated by sexual orientation bias; and 12.7% stemmed from ethnic bias.

Of the 1,415 hate crime offenses based on sexual orientation, 62.3% were classified as anti-male homosexual bias.

Generally hate crime legislation increases the penalties for crimes committed because of race, color, gender, religion, and sexual orientation. Whether a person believes that current criminal and civil statutes are sufficient or that certain criminal acts must be categorized as hate crimes, Wyoming and the country need to serve notice that all human rights will be honored and protected.

The federal Church Arson Protection Act of

Saving the Best of the West in Wyoming

1996 passed to more severely punish those who attack or burn houses of worship. It can serve as a precedent for how the federal government and states can treat hate crimes.

You Don't Need a Weatherman
(to Tell Which Way the Wind Blows)

A signature chapter in the *State of Equality in the Equality State* is nearing its end. It has had many characters, twists, turns, and a frontier sensibility that has been converted into a deep undercurrent of intolerance. Honestly understanding our past and present is the only way to build a road to a more tolerant future.

New laws can help and the better enforcement of existing laws can help even more. Each can stand as a sign that Wyoming will not tolerate any form of discrimination or hate crime. Properly honoring Martin Luther King, Jr. would send a message, too. Telling the truth about our own history and current conditions and then bringing those lessons into the classroom can help better educate a younger generation, and hopefully, help make them more tolerant, as well.

Learning a foreign language and the culture of its native speakers and encouraging travel to more diverse parts of the country or world can help broaden horizons. A recent and encouraging trend at the University of Wyoming shows a growing awareness among students that the world is increasingly interdependent.

In late October, 2008, a report by the University's Office of International Programs revealed a calendar year total of 460 students studying abroad. That reflected a tenfold increase over the last decade. In addition, more students are selecting non-European destinations, including Asia and Africa.

But we also need our university president, elected officials, and religious leaders to speak out and lead us in a more diverse, enlightened, and tolerant direction.

Wyoming, You're So Square, and Baby, I *do* care. We all should.

4

Place Names

Saving the Best of the West in Wyoming

In the "big wonderful" of the American West, a place name stands out as an essential way to give direction and grounding for its citizens and visitors. Place names can also reflect topographical features and history. They set the stage for both ordinary men and women and bigger than life characters such as Lewis and Clark, Sacagawea, Butch Cassidy, the Sundance Kid, and Crazy Horse.

In Wyoming and the rest of the West, we have a seemingly never ending stretch of space which fostered a frontier sensibility that neither restricted freedom nor presumably made anyone better or more special than anyone else.

These legends, the romance, local heroes, and the space have led to a belief in a Western exceptionalism. It is the notion that the West and westerners have a distinct identity and special destiny that is different from other regions of the country. Exceptionalism presumes qualitative difference and superiority to the rest of the world. The Western frontier, its independent way of life, the search for freedom from interference, and the cowboy may have helped forge this conviction.

But make no mistake, Wyoming *is* exceptional. Its natural and almost wonderland beauty is exceptional. Its unlimited space and wildlife are exceptional. Its ever changing light and seasons are exceptional, too. Its land, ranches, and ranchers are exceptional as well. Its explorers and adventurers were exceptional. Its insularity is not.

Just as the Equality State became a myth without a factual foundation, the belief in Western exceptionalism has not adjusted to the real world. Those who are assured of their centrality in the world have been and will be overrun by change.

If we first broaden our glance to national landmarks and their history, then we can quickly put our "exceptionalism" in perspective. Imagine the Grand Canyon: 6 million years old, 18 miles deep and covering 1,217,403 acres. Take a seat in Independence Hall where the Declaration of Independence was adopted on July 4, 1776. Consider Paul Revere's House in Boston, originally built in 1680 where he and his family lived between 1770 to 1800 and from where he started his famous "midnight ride." Visualize the Statue of Liberty standing more than 150 feet tall in New York Harbor commissioned by the French in 1876 to celebrate the centennial of the American Declaration of Independence, and finally dedicated ten years later on October 28, 1886. Every landmark has its special place in history. Some are truly national and international landmarks. Others fade away into local lore.

It is now time to refocus on Wyoming's place names and their assumed singularity. That focus can sharpen our sight of the bigger world that many say "surrounds" us. I prefer to say a bigger world of which we are a special part, but *only* a part. While still holding on to its own sense of place, Wyoming needs to better integrate itself into the whole of national life.

Since it is so easy for Wyomingites and other westerners to embrace their own geography and define the world by it, let's widen the geographic net and explore the true uniqueness of Wyoming place names. This broader exploration is based on the U.S. Geologic Survey's Names Information System.

For example, my home in Wyoming lies just east of the Wyoming Range, the state's namesake mountains and along Horse Creek named by Thomas Fitzpatrick, fur trader mountain man, exceptional guide, and Indian agent.

When trapping beaver along north Horse Creek in April, 1824, twenty Shoshone warriors stole Fitzpatrick's horses. Although he later recovered his horses, the name, Horse Creek, stuck. How special is our Horse Creek? Across the United States 371 streams carry the name Horse Creek. Horse Creeks stretch from New York to California and 38 states in between.

Wyoming has 28 Horse Creeks running through 17 different counties. Texas claims 26 and Oregon 23, while Indiana, Iowa, Maryland, and Michigan each have just 1.

Saving the Best of the West in Wyoming

Earlier, I briefly described the authenticity of Sheridan, Wyoming, and the appeal of its slogan, the *Best of the West*. The residents of Sheridan may be surprised to learn that 31 towns in the United States are named Sheridan. They stretch from Maine to California. Many are located in the Midwest. Each Sheridan has its special history, unique places, and boasts the loyalty of its citizens.

Let's jump up to Teton County, Wyoming, and one of its identifiable features, Dog Creek. Of course, Teton County has 3 of them running through Burnt Mountain, Sheep Mountain, and Munger Mountain, but the rest of the United States contains 108 Dog Creeks. Since we are near the resort town of Jackson, Wyoming, how special is that name? The answer? *Not very.* The U.S. has 41 of them.

Even Wyoming's state capitol city, Cheyenne, has three competitors—Cheyenne in Osborne County, Kansas; another Cheyenne in Roger Mills County, Oklahoma, and the third in Winkler County, Texas.

However, the country has only one Laramie— Laramie, Wyoming, and three cheers for that special place and the University of Wyoming.

Now how about Rock Springs, Wyoming, in Sweetwater County? In 1861, a Pony Express rider, who detoured to avoid Indians, discovered the springs after which the town was named. In 1866, a stage station, stone cabin, and bridge were built at that same location. Later, and located on the Union Pacific rail line and its coal mines, Rock Springs became a magnet for

European immigrants including Italians, Greeks, Russians, Finns and the Irish.

Rock Springs sounds like a different place, but guess again. Our country has 34 Rock Springs and many are located in the south and southwest, and those states include Georgia, Alabama, Arkansas, Kentucky, North Carolina, Florida, Tennessee, New Mexico, and Texas.

What about Cody, Wyoming? Founded in 1896 and named in honor of William F. "Buffalo Bill" Cody, the small western town is the eastern gateway to Yellowstone National Park and the home of the Buffalo Bill Historical Center. It claims to be the "Rodeo Capitol of the World," and is a center for Western art, antiques, and furniture. It is distinct—just like the 8 other towns named Cody. They sprang up in Arizona, Florida, Missouri, Nebraska, Oklahoma, Virginia, Illinois, and Texas.

On one hand, the realization that my Horse Creek or your Cody or Rock Springs also name similar features of many other communities can be humbling, and even more so when these Wyoming landmarks are more local lore than center points of American history. But on the other hand, it is a reminder that we are part of a bigger world—a world that can offer us much and help break down Wyoming's isolation. This realization can also illuminate the truly special character of Wyoming, including its beauty, unbroken space, and history, if honestly told.

Saving the Best of the West in Wyoming

5

Odds and Ends

Saving the Best of the West in Wyoming

These bits and pieces of Wyoming life will reintroduce, from different perspectives, the idea that the state is "just a little off-key." Even though people who live in Wyoming and other states may find this motley assortment of things very odd, they can astonish and amuse.

Wild Lands

Especially in light of the state's very small population, the wildlife and wild lands of Wyoming give the state a near peerless quality. Due to changing landscapes, seasons, and light, they never lose their attraction and mystery for residents and visitors alike. They rightfully earn Wyoming the moniker, the *Big Wonderful.*

The explosion of the natural gas industry, the increase in the number of vacation homes, helter-skelter development, and the subdivision of ranches into ranchettes conspire to threaten open space, ecologically sensitive lands, air quality, and wildlife. The health of wildlife serves as a barometer for the health of the ecosystem, and both are at risk in parts of the state.

In recent years, the energy industry, federal agencies, state government, towns, land trusts, environmental groups, researchers, and ranchers have launched a dizzying array of measures to either mitigate adverse environmental effects or preserve open space and unique places. I applaud these initiatives and others should, too. At the same time, some of these efforts lack a larger vision and may be working on the margins of a problem and ignoring the core.

Most consequential is the fact that not all landscapes, watersheds, airsheds, and ecologies are equally as important and threatened. Further, not all players in the game have the same leverage. For example, private landowners and the Department of Interior's Bureau of Land Management own just about 80% of Wyoming's land. Private landowners possess over half of the state's total land area, and BLM owns just less than 30%. Next, although smaller land owners, the U.S. Forest Service and the state of Wyoming control some of the most precious property. Together they account for over 15% of the state, and the USFS accounts for almost all of that.

These facts bring forth a few consequences. First, Wyoming needs a land use and ecological inventory of the state and a ranking of areas that immediately need more protection than others. If Wyoming's state geologist can map the state's sub-terrain looking for formations suitable for carbon sequestration, the state can certainly manage a surface ecological inventory, including air and water quality. This task seems well suited to a collaborative program between the Wyoming

Saving the Best of the West in Wyoming

Game and Fish Department and the University of Wyoming's Haub School and Ruckelshaus Institute of Environment and Natural Resources. Led by U.S. Geological Survey, the Southwestern Wyoming Landscape Conservation Initiative offers an early model for such an inventory. While focused on oil and gas development and its impact on wildlife species and habitat, in the future it does plan a more complete natural resource inventory and monitoring program.

Yet any assessment needs to recognize that the state and region face some very big problems. They include a long-term drought. A recent study in the journal, *Science,* showed that the persistent decline in the snowpack of western mountains is *not* attributable to natural causes, but to global warming.

Using data collected over the past fifty years, scientists led by Tim Barnett of the Scripps Institution of Oceanography and the University of California at San Diego, confirmed that the mountains of the West are getting more rain, less snow, and the snowpack is breaking up faster. This means less water for power and irrigation in those states, and Mexico, who are members of the Colorado River Compact.

Reaching similar conclusions, Stanford University scientist, Sarah McMenamin, reported in the October 27, 2008 issue of the *Proceedings of the National Academy of Sciences* that even in the protected environs of Yellowstone National Park, four species of amphibians, including frogs, are in severe decline. Since frogs can breathe and drink through their skin, this permeability makes them vulnerable to environmental change. Consequently, they are bellwethers for overall environmental degradation. She also noted, "There is no other reason (than climate change) for the regional aquifer to be drying up."

As other states such as California mandate reductions in carbon dioxide emissions, those states' concerns about global warming will place Wyoming's conventional coal exports to out of state utilities and others at considerable risk. For example, in mid-November, 2008, the Environmental Protections Agency's Appeals Board withdrew a permit for a coal-fired plant in Vernal, Utah. That withdrawal was based on the failure of EPA's regional office to assess and then control carbon dioxide emissions. Almost one hundred proposed coal-fired power plants may now be required to cut their greenhouse emissions and help mitigate global warming.

In the face of these unambiguous threats, the citizens of Wyoming and the West still believe global warming will only seriously affect people who live on the coasts of the United States or states adjacent to them. On Monday, September 22, 2008, Steve Gray, the state's climatologist, cited a recent Mason-Dixon poll when he spoke at the Stroock Forum on Wyoming Lands and People hosted by the University of Wyoming. He said the poll, which surveyed a sample of 400 voters each in Wyoming, Colorado, Arizona, Nevada, and Utah, found that "57% of Wyoming residents and 51% of Westerners think global warming is a bigger threat to those who live elsewhere." Instead, he said, Wyoming is "extremely vulnerable to climate change, no matter the cause."

Even if precipitation levels in Wyoming do not decline as temperatures increase, Gray said, "higher than average temperatures of 1-2° Celsius could reduce the amount of water available for the latter part of the growing season." This scenario would create earlier and faster runoff of water stored as snow in the high mountains and cause more of the state's precipitation to fall as rain instead of snow.

Gray went on to say, "Wyoming is the fifth driest state in the nation. Most water comes from snowpack stored on 7% of the state's land—the high mountains. Thus, we have all of our eggs in one basket." He added, "Wyoming sits at the top of major watersheds, including the Colorado River Basin, which means, a drought has greater impact on the state because shortages here cannot be buffered by extra precipitation elsewhere in the watershed."

Aside from the urgency of facing up to big problems, the scale of Wyoming's private land ownership ensures that one approach to conservation and preservation will have the biggest impact. Ranchers, who properly manage their own property and work as good stewards of the land and water, can dramatically enhance the quality of their environment and its productivity. In fact, maintaining the productivity of their land is in their own self interest.

For example, each year in conjunction with other partners such as the Wyoming Stock Growers Association, the Sand County Foundation gives the Leopold Conservation Award to the one Wyoming ranch that demonstrates extraordinary achievement in conservation. Those conservation practices foster an environmentally and economically sustainable ranch and serve to inspire other ranches to utilize similar practices. The Award includes statewide recognition and a $10,000 gift.

In 2007, the Golden Willow Ranch near Riverton, Wyoming, won, and in 2008, the Pape Ranches in Daniel, Wyoming, were the winner. The Sand County Foundation also gives a similar award to ranches or farms in five other states including Wisconsin, Nebraska, Colorado, and Texas.

The voluntary conservation practices and recognition are laudatory and inspiring, but more ranches could follow those examples if simple state tax and direct financial incentives were designed to encourage and reward them.

Through the donation of conservation easements, land trusts can and do preserve sizable chunks of ranchland and open space in perpetuity. When a landowner donates an easement to a land trust, he or she continues to own the property, but ensures that it can't be subdivided or otherwise developed. The land owners may also reap federal tax or other financial benefits.

Today, five Wyoming communities have local land trusts, and three land trusts operate statewide. The statewide land trusts are the Conservation Fund, the Nature Conservancy's Wyoming Field Office, and the Wyoming Stock

Saving the Best of the West in Wyoming

Growers Agricultural Land Trust. The virtues of conservation easements are that they are tangible, measurable, and voluntary.

Each land trust or their financial backers have and will place a specific number of acres under conservation easements. For example, in 2008, the Nature Conservancy's Wyoming Field Office preserved 11,000 acres. The Wyoming Stock Growers Agricultural Land Trust has placed just over 106,000 acres of ranchland under conservation easements, and one local trust, the Green River Valley Land Trust has preserved 25,000 acres of ranchland. Another local land trust, the Jackson Hole Land Trust, has preserved just over 17,000 acres. In a few short years, together these land trusts have preserved almost 160,000 acres of ranchland—about one half the size of Teton National Park. As time goes by, the number of acres preserved by these land trusts will grow.

Tax and financial incentives for ranchers who are committed environmental stewards and conservation easements can accelerate ranchland and open space preservation, particularly in environmentally critical areas such as migration corridors and pristine rivers and lakes.

Our next focus will be on the energy industry's programs that currently operate mainly on BLM land, except where the companies own the mineral leases on private land. Aside from the mitigation and reclamation requirements imposed by BLM as part of their "Record of Decision" stipulated in the environmental impact statements, individual companies or a consortium of companies often take additional steps that are also incorporated into BLM's final decision.

Most recently, in the late fall of 2008, BLM approved 4,400 new wells on the Pinedale Anticline, including a $34 million mitigation fund underwritten by Questar, Shell, and Ultra. Prior to that fund, the most dramatic financial initiative had been EnCana Oil and Gas (USA) and BP America's contribution of $24 million to an on and off-site mitigation program. That donation was tied to BLM's 2006 approval of EnCana and BP's 3,100 new wells in the Jonah Field south of Pinedale, Wyoming.

The money is, in effect, held in escrow by the state created Wildlife and Natural Resources Trust, and spent according to recommendations of a joint state and federal interagency group.

After a slow and confusing start in 2006, the Jonah Interagency Mitigation and Reclamation Office (JIO) found a wild land conservation strategy that by 2009 has placed almost 12,000 acres of ecologically important private ranchland in Sublette County under conservation easements. Reflecting that workable vision, so far the JIO has spent 42%, or $5,524,171 of its $13,298,930 on conservation easements.

A total of $16.5 million was set aside for wildlife preservation and conservation easements. By committing another $5 million, the JIO also helped preserve another 19,000 acres of two historic ranches along 4.5 miles of the Green River. If, during the next few years, the JIO spends another $2 million on ranchland conservation, it will have contributed enormously to the preservation of open space, wildlife habitat, migration corridors, streams, rivers, and the overall quality of life in Sublette County.

If the new $34 million mitigation fund follows suit, it can turn the corner on ensuring a quality environment, better citizen access to natural resources, and a new and sustainable economy whose linchpins are Wyoming ranches

The BLM's ability and willingness to ensure multiple-use and ecological integrity is primarily a function of the federal administration in power and the price of oil.

The Bush Administration promoted energy development, often at the expense of multiple-use options and the environment. Since Sublette County now produces 40% of Wyoming's natural gas, the dilemmas faced by other parts of Wyoming, Colorado, and Utah are mirror images of the development in Sublette County.

The Environmental Protection Agency first graded the BLM's early 2008 draft Environmental Impact Statement governing year around drilling on the Pinedale Anticline or the Mesa as a failure. EPA labeled it "environmentally unsatisfactory/ inadequate information." The BLM virtually ignored air and water quality standards.

For example, nitrous oxide emissions in the area were five times the threshold BLM set in 2000 for the same airshed. Further, air pollution was affecting the Class I viewsheds in the Wind River Range Wilderness. With respect to water quality, BLM ignored monitoring data that showed energy production contaminated an aquifer used as a drinking water source, and that benzene, a known carcinogen, and other hydrocarbons had been detected in 88 of approximately 230 water wells monitored. This sorry record stands in sharp contrast to the conservation ethic that guides the Jonah Interagency Office and includes BLM in the leadership role.

As if such malfeasance wasn't bad enough, on February 21-22, 2008 and then again on March 9,10,11, 23 (Easter Sunday) and 24, 2008, the ozone levels in Sublette County dramatically exceeded the Environmental Protection Agency's National Ambient Air Quality Standard of 80 (ppb) parts per billion. Some of the air quality monitoring stations recorded eight-hour averages as high as 122 ppb. Ozone, a harmful irritant that causes respiratory problems in children, the elderly, and others with breathing issues, is most commonly associated with the Los Angeles Basin and the Washington, D.C. metropolitan area.

Since the 80 ppb standard did not alleviate the respiratory problems elsewhere, the EPA recently lowered the standard to 75 ppb. Wyoming's Department of Environmental Quality issued its first ozone advisory one week after the first episode of excessive levels. DEQ records showed excessive ozone levels as early as 2005. However, no current air quality model would have predicted these levels in a rural mountain region historically known for its pristine air. Those models have been based on summer experiences in large metropolitan areas such as Denver.

On April 21, 2008, the Wyoming Department

of Environmental Quality, authorized by the EPA to monitor and manage air and water quality in Wyoming, held a public meeting to provide more background and proposed solutions to ozone levels in the Upper Green River Valley's water and air shed. Almost two hundred people attended.

Wyoming's DEQ agreed to install another air quality monitoring station in the town of Pinedale, and in conjunction with the Sublette County Commission, to undertake a toxicity study that can evaluate ozone's health effects. The DEQ promised to return to Sublette County and report on its progress with BLM and the industry. It has fulfilled that promise.

In the meantime a citizen's group initially known by the acronym CLOUD formed and continued its protests and educational forums. Regional and national media renewed their attention to the pollution of otherwise clear air and clean water.

Prodded by the Wyoming DEQ and CLOUD, the Bureau and Land Management and the Pinedale Anticline operators have taken stronger measures to improve air quality, water quality and the regular monitoring of both. Only time will reveal the impact of these initiatives. But Wyoming has every reason to expect better stewardship of federally-owned public lands under the Obama Administration.

In the latest development on March 12, 2009, Wyoming's Governor, Dave Freudenthal, requested that the Environmental Protection Agency designate Sublette County and parts of other counties as an ozone nonattainment area. Since new monitoring data and air quality analysis has shown a persistent measure of ozone, this action was justified. Even though the Wyoming Department of Environmental Quality has worked aggressively with energy companies to mitigate ozone levels, a nonattainment designation will require the state to develop a plan that will specify the measures it will take to return the area to attainment status.

Our next stop is another state agency in Wyoming. In 2005, the Wyoming Legislature created the Wyoming Wildlife and Natural Resources Trust. It is funded by interest earned on a permanent account which is provided by legislative appropriations. That permanent account holds $57 million and received an additional $35 million in 2008-2009. The $57 million has produced about $3 million in interest and the $92 million could yield about $5 million. Most of that interest is used to fund projects designed to improve wildlife habitat or natural resource values. It is guided by a nine member citizens' board.

Since 2006, the Trust spent around $8 million. It measures success by expenditures, the funded project's ability to attract other matching funds, and the number of projects. Unlike the conservation strategy supported by EnCana and BP's $24 million, the Trust has mostly opted for discreet projects from county to county.

For example, in the Teton, Sublette, and Fremont Counties' cluster, the Trust has underwritten a five acre pond for waterfowl, installed a fish screen on an irrigation ditch, improved two stream channels, improved a wetland, and helped place flashing signs that warn Jackson Hole motorists of large animal migration or their presence in high traffic corridors.

Each of these individual projects may have merit, but they constitute a piecemeal approach. It is impossible to determine their impact on Wyoming's natural resources or wildlife, and they do not represent a long term strategy that can leverage major change or solve the bigger problems. Nonetheless, the Trust takes great pains to point out that it has at least one project in each of Wyoming's 23 counties.

As a possible harbinger of a more measurable and comprehensive approach, in late 2008, the Trust committed $1.2 million—by far its largest contribution to date—to help purchase conservation easements on the two historic ranches along the Green River in Sublette County. These are the same ranches supported by the JIO's $5 million noted earlier.

Nowhere can the cacophony of government agencies, energy companies, nonprofits and trusts be better heard than in the case of the greater sage grouse, perhaps the most thoroughly assessed bird in the world.

First, and incorporating the views of a citizens' working group, we have in hand the Wyoming Game and Fish Department's *Greater Sage Grouse Conservation Plan* issued in July, 2003. It cited and used eighteen separate research papers or studies on the greater sage grouse. Those who follow the greater sage grouse must have thought, "at last a definitive plan based on research and common sense." Not so, two years later the U.S. Department of Interior's U.S. Geologic Survey produced a first class *Range-Wide Conservation Assessment for the Greater Sage Grouse and Sagebrush Habitat* that included a detailed assessment of the predicament faced by the greater sage grouse in Wyoming.

This plan also included the creation of local working groups to follow up on the assessments. Oddly enough, the assessments appear to have been ignored by USGS's sister agency, BLM, as it has proceeded willy-nilly approving gas wells in sagebrush habitat.

All plans, studies, and assessments are very clear—the sagebrush habitat is declining, and so is the sage grouse population. The *Conservation Assessment* concludes, "We are not optimistic about the future of sage grouse because of the long-term population declines coupled with the continued degradation of habitat and other factors (including West Nile Virus)."

In the face of this thorough assessment and stark warning, in 2005, Shell Exploration and Production donated $1 million to create the Tom Thorne Sage Grouse Conservation Fund to further research on the sage grouse in the Upper Green River Basin and promote citizen education.

Much of the initial sage grouse research was designed to avoid an Endangered Species listing. But despite the potentially fatal peril facing the bird, three years later we are still studying the problem, degrading sagebrush habitat, ignoring climate change, and putting band-aids on an ecological hemorrhage.

Dog Fighting

Let's take a ringside seat at the 2008 dog fighting spectacle in the Wyoming Legislature. In the event that time has erased your memory or part of it, in 2007, Michael Vick, superstar and quarterback for the Atlanta Falcons, was convicted on federal felony charges related to his role in an interstate dog fighting ring known as the Bad Newz Kennels. Three other co-defendants were also convicted. On December 10, 2007, Vick was sentenced to twenty-three months in federal prison followed by three years of probation.

A separate trial could have been set in Virginia to try Vick under state law, and he could have served up to another ten years in a state penitentiary. He was suspended from the NFL, lost $20 million of a $30 million dollar bonus, lost his endorsement contracts, was forced to liquidate many of his real estate assets, and finally declared bankruptcy. In late November 2008, and after Vick pleaded guilty to a single count of dog fighting, his sentence under Virginia law was suspended.

However, Vick's case became a major and sustained media event and highlighted the state laws and penalties for dog fighting. In late 2007, only two states in the U.S. treated dog fighting as misdemeanor punishable by up to six months in jail and no more than a $750 fine. Those states were Wyoming and Idaho. In early 2008, the Idaho Legislature voted to make dog fighting a felony. When Idaho finally passed its legislation, it joined 48 other states which already punished dog fighting as a felony. Wyoming was the single exception.

While the state had no evidence that dog fighting was a problem in Wyoming, the debate hit the legislature in early 2008. The first round debated whether or not the current animal cruelty laws which include felony provisions were sufficient to discourage dog fighting. The second round went to those who advocated a bill that would make the second dog fighting offense a felony. When their bill was labeled a "feel good measure," they threatened to amend the bill and make the first offense a felony.

On February 21, 2008, the Wyoming House voted 52 to 2 and sent a bill to the Senate that would make the first offense a felony.

The Senate also passed the bill, and the

governor signed the bill that included a felony provision for cockfighting, as well. The maximum penalty for dogfighting or cockfighting will be a year in prison and a $5,000 fine. Much of this spectacle was designed to manage an "image," problem, and now the state has something to crow about.

Ironically, by managing this problem, Wyoming gained the distinction as the state where the penalties for dog fighting and cockfighting are more severe than for cases of domestic abuse and violence. Today, the battery, or beating, of a household member is a misdemeanor and again punishable by up to six months in jail and a fine of up to $750. That anomaly qualifies Wyoming for a moral knock-out punch.

Drinking

Let's rev up our time machine again and set it for Cheyenne, Wyoming, on February 22, 2007. We must brace ourselves for another remarkable chapter in Wyoming social history. After decades of allowing drivers and passengers to have open containers of alcholic beverages in moving vehicles, the Wyoming House courageously voted 52 to 7 to ban all open containers in moving vehicles. Before the end of the 2007 legislative session, the Senate passed a similar bill, and the governor signed it.

While drunk driving has long been illegal, until the 21st Century Wyoming drivers could legally drink while driving. During this period, Wyoming stood by and watched as 59% of all traffic fatalities in the state were alcohol related, and a stunning 52% involved individuals who were legally drunk, if not well above the legal limit.

Wyoming's bold legislative action in 2007 served to preserve its federal highway funding, and over time it may contribute to an absolute drop in alcohol related traffic deaths. However, today, first, second, and third drunk driving offenses are treated as misdemeanors. Only if an individual has four offenses within five years will he or she be treated as a felon. If the DUI offenses involve bodily injury or death, the penalties and felony charges jump.

In early 2008, the Wyoming legislature considered "boosting" these penalties so that a third offense in seven years would qualify as a felony and a fifth DUI in a lifetime would also qualify as a felony. The House passed the bill, but in early March, the Senate killed it with no debate. The 2009 legislature also buried legislation that would have raised drunk driving penalties.

After the 2008 legislation withered, the April 16, 2008 edition of the *Jackson Hole News and Guide* reported that a forty-four year old man was arrested on the suspicion of driving under the influence for the fifteenth time. Since he was charged with a felony, this DUI must have been his fourth in five years, but he was driving drunk at least eleven times with only minor penalties, if any.

A November, 2008 study by the Wyoming Association of Sheriffs and Police Chiefs found that of 21,758 arrests between October 1, 2007 and September 30, 2008, alcohol played a role in

Saving the Best of the West in Wyoming

70.65%. Further, it discovered that "driving under the influence" accounted for 37.5% of all arrests or about four out of ten. Even more remarkable was the finding that the average reported blood alcohol content (BAC) for DUI arrests statewide was 0.158. In Wyoming, a person driving with a blood alcohol content of 0.08 is legally impaired.

In other words, the average drunk driver arrested in Wyoming had a BAC almost 200% of the state's legal definition of drunk driving.

Even though the details of the drunk driving laws vary from state-to-state, twenty-two states treat a third DUI offense as a felony. Many others also suspend driver licenses and install ignition interlock systems.

For example, Texas treats third time drunk drivers as felons with a minimum of two years and up to ten years in the state penitentiary. Upon release, their drivers' licenses are suspended for two years, and they later may be required to install an ignition interlock device at their own expense.

Although the 2009 Wyoming Legislature failed to raise the penalties for drunk driving, it did pass a bill that will require ignition interlocks on the vehicles of all repeat offenders and first time offenders with a BAC of .15 or higher.

If avoidable, my family and I never travel on the roads after 10 p.m.

A Health Check-Up

The last part of *Odds and Ends* looks at the health of Wyoming residents, and it is proper to end on a higher note with some better news. Although initially the score may have a macabre tonality, it is still upbeat information, and data that might even surprise Wyoming natives.

First, heart disease is the leading killer in the United States and in Wyoming. It accounts for 27% of all deaths in the U.S. and 24% of all deaths in Wyoming. But the national age-adjusted death rate per 100,000 is 217, and in Wyoming it is 187.6—considerably less.

In a similar vein, cancer is the second leading cause of death in the United States and in Wyoming. Nationwide, cancer accounts for

Saving the Best of the West in Wyoming

23% of all deaths and 22% of all deaths in Wyoming. The national age-adjusted death rate is 185.8 per 100,000 population, and in Wyoming, it is 172.7. Further, out of the 38 states that saw declines in cancer mortality rates between 2003 and 2004, Wyoming witnessed the biggest decline of 17.3%.

When it comes to chronic lower respiratory disease such as emphysema, bronchitis and asthma the notes are a little sourer. Chronic lower respiratory disease is the fourth ranking cause of death in the U.S., but the third ranking cause of death in Wyoming. Nationwide this disease accounts for 5% of all deaths, and in Wyoming it accounts for 7.8%. Similarly, accidents or unintentional deaths are the fifth leading cause of death in the United States and the fourth in Wyoming. Nationally, accidents account for around 5% of all deaths and 6.1% in Wyoming. The prevalence of mining, construction, and agriculture in Wyoming can go a long way toward explaining this disparity.

On a host of other measures that gauge general health and well being such as AIDS, Alzheimer cases, both adult and high school student smoking rates, new cancer cases, tuberculosis, obesity rates, hypertension, and diabetes, Wyoming performs better than the national average. In AIDS, diabetes, hypertension, and kids who are overweight, Wyoming performs far better than most states.

For example, a 2008 study by the Robert Wood Johnson Foundation and the Trust for America's Health found that Wyoming had the second lowest rate of childhood obesity when compared with rates in all other states. Utah ranked first. Also in late October, 2008, the Center for Disease Control released the results of a study that showed Wyoming had the second lowest rate of diabetes among all states. Minnesota had the lowest.

When it comes to the immunization gap (the number of infants under thirty-four months without all immunizations) and low birth weight babies, Wyoming performs worse than the national average. Also the percentages of all uninsured Wyomingites and Wyoming children are similar to the national averages.

Considering the rural character of Wyoming and the distance of many from a hospital, these health notes are truly high ones.

However, two very dark figures lurk behind the curtain. The first is suicide. Nationwide between 2004 and 2005, (a period when suicide rates were clearly rising when compared to the previous fifteen years) the overall and age-adjusted suicide rate was 10.9 per 100,000 population. During 2004-2005, Wyoming had 17.58 suicides —nearly double the national average. That placed Wyoming in 5th place behind Alaska at 21.29 per 100,000 people, Montana at 20.28, Nevada at 19.53, and New Mexico at 18.36 per 100,000 population.

From 2004-2005 and for *youth ages 15-24*, Wyoming ranked 4th at 16.41 per 100,000 population. Alaska's young adult suicide rate of 34.70 per 100,000 tragically earned a first place. New Mexico followed with 23.97, and in 3rd place ¯

was Montana at 21.16 per 100,000. Nevada was 5th with a 15.27 rate. These state rates compare to the nation's 10.21 youth suicides per 100,000 population.

Although much attention has focused on Wyoming's youth suicide rate, particularly among young men, the state's suicide rate for the elderly, ages 65 years and above, in 2005 stood at a distressing 27.5 per 100,000 and that compares to the U.S. rate of 14.7. Only Nevada, at 35.7 per 100,000 population, ranks higher than Wyoming.

The second dark figure represents the health status of Indian tribes of Wyoming. Whether it is chronic disease, smoking rates, alcohol consumption, obesity, or preventive medicine, the tribes' health is much poorer than their white counterparts.

For example, the Wyoming Department of Health's 1999-2003 Behavior Risk Factor Surveillance System showed that 50.2% of Wyoming Native Americans smoked compared to 22.7% for white non-Hispanics; 28.5% of the Indians binge drank compared to 17.1% of the whites; twice as many Indians had diabetes as did the white non-Hispanics; and 33.6% of the Wyoming tribal members had no health coverage compared to 16% for whites.

I cannot offer a prescription for these haunting figures, except that we Wyomingites can do better.

6

Old Timers
and
Newcomers

Saving the Best of the West in Wyoming

Whether old or new, anyone who lives in Wyoming year-around will inevitably hear or participate in a discussion about whether native Wyoming citizens are more authentic and knowledgeable about Wyoming life, if not "better," than the newcomers. Many newcomers fall victim to this rhetorical trap and seemingly never escape.

For example, when we first moved to Daniel, Wyoming, six years ago, I visited the local liquor store then named Outfitter Liquor, in Pinedale, Wyoming. Just ahead of me at the check-out counter was a working woman dressed in Carhartt bib overalls and jacket. Her hands were calloused, her face windswept, and she looked about forty years old. She was a construction worker, a winter employee at an elk feed ground, or ranch hand. In her own way she was attractive. As she bought her beer, she told the liquor store manager that she had lived in Wyoming for seventeen years, and people still called her a newcomer.

Saving the Best of the West in Wyoming

She said, "If I die here forty years or more from now, they will put on my tombstone, *newcomer, Jane Doe, died in Wyoming.*"

Near mid-February, 2008, the Wyoming Humanities Council published a fifty-five page *Newcomers' Guide* that included information on Wyoming geography, history, cultural traits, and historic bars and hotels. In it we were told that "Wyomingites have a strong sense of sharing a unique past with a certain sense of exclusivity."

We know that its past is unique, and I plan on joining another less exclusive club. The *Guide* goes on to tell us that one of Wyomingites' mannerisms is "an unspoken, yet assumed sense of superiority, and a ready willingness to defend Wyoming against negative comments from outsiders."

A member of the very small audience that attended the *Guide's* unveiling bemoaned that after living in Wyoming for thirty-five years, she was still considered a newcomer.

I began to think that many people may just not want the label, "native." What we really need is *A Newcomer's Guide for Wyoming Old Timers* that can give the natives a lesson on the immigrant history of Wyoming and a tutorial on changing life and attitudes for the better.

When you stop for a moment and think about this competition and the presumed advantage held by the natives, it is even more off the mark. Neither group holds a monopoly on idiocy. Some members of each group are equally limited. Similarly, some in both groups are engaging, hard working, bright, and creative. Next, and except for the true Native Americans, Wyoming and other states in the Rocky Mountain West were all settled by people who came from someplace else, whether it was another state, territory, or country. Otherwise, Wyoming would have never been settled and never achieved statehood. Wyoming and America are first a history of immigrants and only later a history of partial assimilation. Wyoming's immigrant history is just much more recent than most other states, and less studied.

Again we can climb aboard our time machine and meet some of Wyoming's most famous immigrants. One of the keenest of all mountain men, Thomas Fitzpatrick, came from Ireland. John Colter and Jim Bridger, two heroic mountain men, were born and raised in Virginia.

Colter was one of nine young men recruited for the Lewis and Clark expedition. On their return journey, he was released from the expedition and began an almost mythical four years as a mountain man. During a remarkable five hundred mile trip in the winter of 1807-1808, he crossed the Big Horn Basin; explored the upper reaches of the Wind River Range; was the first white man to see Jackson's Hole and the Teton Range; crossed into Pierre's Hole on the west side of the Tetons; walked along the shores of Jackson Lake; and stood at the north edge of Yellowstone Lake where he saw the thermal wonders that later would be called "Colter's Hell."

He was the first white man to explore what would become Yellowstone National Park. Naked and weaponless, he survived a more than two hundred mile race for his life with Blackfeet warriors in chase, and eventually provided William

Saving the Best of the West in Wyoming

Clark detailed geographic knowledge of the Yellowstone River and surrounding areas.

Jim Bridger, known as a teller of tall tales, also enjoyed the reputation as one of the best trappers, guides, and scouts in the Rocky Mountain West. Much of his fur trade and exploration was centered in Wyoming. His mental map of western geography was so vast and detailed that he was later called the "Atlas of the West."

"Old Gabe," as his friends called him, perfectly represented the mountain man of the 1830s. He gained a unique understanding of the land, animals, and Indians, and his bravery was unquestioned. His skill with horses and his rifle were legendary.

Beyond Thomas Fitzpatrick, other immigrants from the British Isles found their way to the fur trading West and life as mountain men or explorers. They included Robert Stuart, Ramsey Crooks, Donald McKenzie, Andrew Drips, Robert Campbell, and William May. Drips and Campbell helped Fitzpatrick manage the American Fur Company and later the Rocky Mountain Fur Company. Of course, and on the heels of Lewis and Clark, Stuart and his party sailed to Astoria, Oregon, while Wilson Price Hunt took the overland route. Crooks and McKenzie were members of Hunt's expedition. Later Stuart returned east by the overland route.

Soon we will meet other famous Wyoming immigrants, but let's fast forward to 1870 and gain a broader understanding of immigrant life in Wyoming Territory. In that year, over 40% of

Wyoming's 9,118 residents were new immigrants. Twenty-five percent of the total population was British, Irish, Scottish or Welsh. Those from the British Isles also represented over half of the foreign-born population. Soon that would change, but by 1880, just shy of 30% of Wyoming's population were new immigrants, and the majority still came from the British Isles.

Most foreign-born and foreign speaking immigrants made interim stops in the United States before landing in Wyoming, which means that when those immigrants arrived they could generally speak English and knew something about the culture and geography of the United States. That helps explain their assimilation.

A quick snapshot of those immigrants shows how "embedded" they were in Wyoming culture. The 1880 Census counted a total state population of only 20,789. It listed 311 "stock growers" and "ranchmen." Of those, 33 were born and raised in Ohio; 29 in New York; 26 in Pennsylvania; 18 in Missouri; 14 in Illinois; 10 were born in both Indiana and Maine; 8 in Maryland and Kentucky; 7 in Iowa; and 2 in Texas. When added together, these immigrant ranchers equal 53% of all cattlemen in the state. Also another 30% of the cattlemen were foreign-born. Only 2 in 10 ranchers had Wyoming roots.

A Few Good Men

Now we can meet some of Wyoming's most famous people. Although it may come as a surprise, some of Wyoming's most prominent men were immigrants—born and raised in another state—and one of them was foreign-born.

Wyoming history has dubbed the first three the "Grand Old Men." Each was a self-made man, who succeeded in business and politics, when few Wyomingites had climbed the ladder of such success. They contributed to Wyoming's early development, but more importantly were seen as part of the romantic West.

The first was Joseph Maull Carey, who was born on January 19, 1845, in Milton, Sussex County, Delaware. His parents were successful farmers and provided Carey with a first class education. After he attended Union College in New York, he entered the University of Pennsylvania Law School and earned his law degree in 1864. He was admitted to the bar in 1867 and began private practice in Philadelphia.

He was also active in Republican Party politics and worked for U.S. Grant's presidential campaign. His reward was an 1869 appointment as the United States attorney for Wyoming Territory, and in 1871, he was appointed as associate justice of Wyoming's Territorial Supreme Court. After that term Carey enjoyed the *nom de plume*, "Judge."

He retired from the bench in 1876, and joined by his brother, Carey began a successful ranching business. However, during this period he served as a member of the United States Centennial Commission and the Republican National Committee. In 1881, he was elected mayor of Cheyenne. Carey was regarded as an astute and able politician and excellent stump speaker.

In 1885, he was elected as a Republican to the first of three terms in the U.S. House of Representatives, where he authored and managed the bill that admitted Wyoming to statehood. He also served as the Chairman of the House Education and Labor Committee. When Wyoming became a state in 1890, the Wyoming Legislature elected him to serve as a United States Senator.

In 1885, and after he was shoved aside by his Republican adversary, Francis Warren, he returned to law practice in Cheyenne. He was elected Governor for a single four year term in

Saving the Best of the West in Wyoming

1911. Breaking with the state's Republican machine, he won election as an "Independent Republican" with the support and endorsement of Wyoming Democrats. In 1912, he also sided with Teddy Roosevelt and the Progressive Party.

Although initially a conservative Republican, he governed in a more progressive tradition. Due to his pursuit of "good government initiatives such as, anti-corruption legislation, the regulation of the securities industry, and agricultural cooperatives," he was regarded as one of Wyoming's most outstanding governors. He died in Cheyenne, Wyoming, on February 4, 1924—fifty-five years after he first set foot on Wyoming Territory.

The next "Grand Old Man" was Francis E. Warren, the Republican nemesis of Judge Carey. Warren, an immigrant, too, was born in Hinsdale, Massachusetts, on June 20, 1844. He served as a private and non-commissioned officer in the Union Army and earned the Medal of Honor. Shortly after the war he took up farming, but in 1886 at the age of twenty-four, he moved to the part of Dakota Territory that within a year would become Wyoming Territory. In 1871, he married Helen M. Smith, also from Hinsdale.

He possessed a remarkable business sense. He built the Warren Livestock Company which by 1889 controlled over 250,000 acres and had 90,000 sheep, 2,500 head of cattle, 2,000 horses, and 2,000 Angora goats.

The Warren Mercantile also grew into one of the largest in Wyoming. Recovering from the 1890s Depression, by the early 1900s he had become the richest man in Wyoming—worth an estimated $5 million. Today, that $5 million is the equivalent of almost $110 million.

Warren was also known for his political acumen. He began his career as a member of the Cheyenne City Council serving in 1873 and 1874. He also served on the Territorial Council and was elected mayor of Cheyenne in 1885. However, in that same year he was appointed territorial governor by President Chester Arthur and appointed to a second term in 1889 by President Benjamin Harrison.

In 1890, he became the first elected governor of Wyoming, but six weeks later the state legislature elected him a U.S. Senator. He served in the U.S. Senate for thirty-seven years and four days. During his almost forty year Senate career he served at different times as chairman of the Senate Appropriations Committee and chairman of the Military Affairs Committee. He used those positions to shower benefits on Wyoming. He was considered a master at dispensing patronage, but also an able legislator.

He was the undisputed leader of the Wyoming Republican Party and the Wyoming delegation to the U.S. Congress. At the age of eighty-five he died in Washington D.C., on November 24, 1929— fifty-six years after his arrival in Wyoming. At the time of his death he was planning his next election campaign. He was buried in Cheyenne.

The third "Grand Old Man," John B. Kendrick, appears as the most colorful of the three. The youngest son of a Texas pioneer family, John Benjamin Kendrick was born on September 6, 1857,

Saving the Best of the West in Wyoming

in Cherokee County, Texas. His father worked as a cotton farmer and his mother, who was born in Ireland, worked beside him. They died young, leaving John and his sister, Rosa, orphans, who lived with Texas relatives.

At the age of fifteen, Kendrick found his first real job breaking horses in exchange for room and board. At twenty-two, he hired on with the Snyder-Wulfjen Brothers from Round Rock, Texas. Like the other cowboys, he helped trail cattle from Matagorda Bay on the Gulf of Mexico to the northeastern Wyoming grasslands. Using his cowboy wages, he bought a few head of cattle and let them graze with the Wulfjen herd. During this time he also avoided gambling and drinking and spent his spare time learning to read and write. Somewhat later he married Wulfjen's daughter, Eula.

By 1882, Charles Wulfjen's holdings were absorbed by the Converse Cattle Company, and Kendrick profited by selling his cattle to them. With that profit he began to build his own herd, and in 1887, he signed on to run the Converse Cattle Company. By 1889, he had moved the entire operation from eastern Wyoming to south-central Montana.

In 1895, Kendrick completed his purchase of the company and built a ranching empire that consisted of over 200,000 acres in southern Montana and northern Wyoming. It was known as the OW ranch. By then Kendrick had settled in Sheridan, Wyoming, and spent many years helping build the city, including his mansion, "Trails End."

Unlike Carey and Warren, Kendrick was a Democrat. He broke into politics through his election to the Wyoming Senate in 1910. In 1913, he ran against incumbent Senator Francis Warren, and lost. But he gained public recognition and respect. He then won the governorship in 1914—a rare break from Wyoming's emerging Republican majority.

After two years as governor, he ran for the U.S Senate and became the first Senator from Wyoming elected by popular vote. He served two more terms and, not surprisingly, was an advocate for cattlemen's interests. Since he missed his ranch and family, he announced in 1932 that he would not seek re-election the next year. In fall, 1933, at age seventy-six, he suddenly died from a cerebral hemorrhage.

His legacy was his drive, ambition, and love of ranching. He resided in Wyoming for fifty-five years, and I doubt that earlier in his life anyone called him a newcomer.

Although many famous and not so famous Wyoming citizens were and are immigrants, our last notable immigrant was also foreign-born. He was Count Otto Franc von Lichtenstein, a German nobleman and better known as Otto Franc. He was born in Germany in August, 1846, and at age twenty immigrated to the U.S.

After an 1877 hunting trip in the Big Horn Basin, Franc returned in 1879, and established one of Wyoming's most famous ranches, the Pitchfork. The ranch is located on the Upper Greybull River near present day Meeteetse. Franc built a ranch so large that history calls him a "cattle baron," and he also served as a sheriff and judge.

Living in Meeteetse at the same time as Franc was Robert Leroy Parker, later known as Butch Cassidy. Parker and Franc became antagonists, and in the early 1890s, Franc swore out a warrant for the arrest of Parker and his friend, Al Hainer, on charges of horse stealing. Both were arrested near Auburn in present day Lincoln County by Uinta County Deputy Sheriffs Bob Calverly and John Chapman.

Parker was convicted and sent to the Wyoming State Penitentiary. Hainer was acquitted, and many thought that his acquittal was due to a deal with Franc that sold out his friend, Parker. After serving two years, Parker was pardoned by then Governor William Richards. Parker returned to Meeteetse where in 1894, Franc swore out another warrant for his arrest. The resolution of that warrant is unclear.

It was also rumored that Franc helped bankroll the "regulators" during the Johnson County War that pitted the big ranchers against the homesteaders. Still shrouded in mystery, Franc died in 1903 from a gunshot wound. Could it have been Butch Cassidy?

At that stage in the Pitchfork's history a wealthy stockbroker, Louis Graham Phelps, purchased the ranch. Charles Josiah Belden, whose California family was also very wealthy, was a friend of Phelps' son, Eugene, and they frequently visited the ranch.

In 1912 Belden married Eugene's sister, Frances, and later began taking photographs of life on the Pitchfork. Most of his images were taken during the 1920s and 1930s, and this setting provided the background for some of the classic photos of ranch and cowboy life.

When Louis Phelps died in 1922, the ranch was willed to Belden and Eugene Phelps. Ranch management was not the strong point for either, and in 1940, Belden and Frances divorced. Belden married again and moved to Florida where in 1966, he died of a self-inflicted gunshot wound. However, today the Pitchfork thrives under even newer owners.

Beyond these notables, better known Wyoming personalities were also immigrants. Buffalo Bill Cody was born and raised in Iowa. Butch Cassidy was born in Utah, and James Cash Penney, who launched his nationwide chain of department stores in Kemmerer, Wyoming, was born in Missouri.

The Infamous and Just Ordinary

Since our time machine is hovering near the late 1800s, let's take a closer look at the different immigrant groups that came to Wyoming. Although citizens from many foreign lands have been represented in Wyoming's population, the main ethnic groups or foreign-born immigrants came from Europe and then only from a handful of countries. We already know that in the 1870s and 1880s the immigrants from the British Isles were the dominate group and left a sizable imprint on Wyoming life.

The Britons represented over eighty different occupations, from cattle baron and ranch hand to miner, banker, and prostitute. Even a Scotsman by birth and a defeated candidate for governor of

Kansas, Thomas Moonlight, was appointed Wyoming's territorial governor by President Grover Cleveland in 1887.

Beyond the adventurers, the two occupations that attracted more Britons than any others were mining and ranching. Since they spoke English and had mining experience in their homelands, they prospered in the mining business.

In the late 1870s and 1880s and still feeling the pulse of empire, the English and Scots poured money and men into the Wyoming cattle business. Ranches such as the Swan Land and Cattle Company, the Dakota Stock and Grazing Company, and the Powder River Cattle Company owned thousands of acres, cattle, and horses. Expecting quick profits, investment grew at a rapid pace. By 1885, 1.5 million cattle were roaming the Wyoming range compared with 500,000 just six years earlier. In that same year, the same number of Wyoming cattle were grazing in neighboring states. Due to a dry summer in 1886 and the severe winter of 1886-1887, the next decade saw most British cattle companies collapse.

Some fascinating and eccentric Britons marked this era of British hegemony. Sir Moreton Frewen, who ranched on the Powder River, and Lionel Sartoris, who ranched near Laramie, built opulent baronial manors staffed by valets, butlers, maids, and chefs. They continued the traditional hunts with hounds, horses, and costumes, but beyond foxes they chased coyotes, wolves, and antelope. They even built horse racing tracks on their properties and spent small fortunes for their most prized race horses.

Moreton Frewen and his brother, Richard, whose brand was the 76, ran 60,000 cattle on their ranch. They literally owned a "kingdom." They hosted hunting parties in the fall and house parties in the summer. So that their guests and the flowers for them might arrive with god's speed, they set up relay stations up to 250 miles south of the ranch. Horses would then bring the guests and flowers in on a gallop.

On the other extreme was Clement S. "Ben" Benough, who received a healthy stipend or "remittance" from his wealthy English family and lived in the utter isolation of the Laramie Plains. He gained a reputation for boxing with bears, receiving staggering amounts of mail from home, and using Siberian wolfhounds to chase coyotes. He never returned to Britain and never claimed his rightful inheritance. He lived and died in a dilapidated cabin.

Even more tragic is the tale of Harry Thynne. He came from impeccable English nobility, including the Duke of Somerset, but later was cast off by his "bibulous" parents. He traveled west, and Harry briefly worked as a cowboy for Sir Moreton Frewen. He apparently had no affinity for the cowboy life, and began a mediocre career as a writer. However, he excelled at drinking whiskey and soon shot himself to death.

In the early 1900s, the Montcreiffe and Wallop families joined together and brought polo to the area near Sheridan, Wyoming, and Oliver Henry Wallop's grandson, Malcolm Wallop, who was born in New York City and attended Yale University, defeated incumbent Democrat, Gale McGee, in 1976, and was elected to the U.S. Senate. He served three terms. He currently splits his time between Wyoming and the East coast.

Although the British—and particularly, the Irish—maintained their dominate position into the 1880s, German immigration accelerated during that time. In 1870, Germans accounted for 19% of the new and foreign-born immigrants and 7% of the total population. By 1900, over 2,000 Germans lived in Wyoming and due to a later wave of Russian-Germans, the number doubled by 1920.

The rising fortunes of the cattle business attracted most of the first and second generation Germans who migrated to Wyoming. About 20% of native Germans came directly to Wyoming. Thirty percent migrated five years after their arrival in the U.S., and another 30% did not cross the Wyoming borders for 10 to 20 years. Since over 60% of the German immigrants already spoke English and had learned some American customs, their assimilation into Wyoming culture was more rapid than some other native Europeans.

Beyond ranching and farming, Wyoming Germans worked or owned restaurants, bakeries, butcher and cheese-making shops, and breweries. Almost every Wyoming town of any size had a brewery, and the Sweetwater Brewery in Green River was managed by Hugo M. Gaenssler and enjoyed a state and region wide reputation for superior beer. It mainly operated from 1875-1920 and won recognition at two world fairs.

Among the early German immigrants were a small number of German Jews, and many settled in Cheyenne. In 1888, they were able to build their first temple, Temple Emanuel.

Recently, Jews have accounted for only about 0.1% of the total population, or today about 532 self-identified Jews.

World War I and World War II prompted some hostility toward Wyoming Germans, and their immigration slowed dramatically. By 1950, German natives accounted for less than 1% of Wyoming's total population, but they had contributed enormously to its economy and social life.

Prior to 1910, the Britons, Germans, Scandinavians, and Chinese defined Wyoming's immigrant population, but in 1910, 1,961 came from Italy; 1,915 from Greece; 1,575 from Japan; 437 from Hungary; and 3,966 from Austria, but that included people from Austria,Czechoslovakia, and Yugoslavia.

Many of these later immigrants came to work in the mines or for the railroads, and then later worked in the trades, businesses or politics. Similar to the Germans, few immigrated directly to Wyoming, and before entering Wyoming most had lived in other states. Each brought with them their traditions and religions. However, where ethnic communities and traditions can thrive in large cities, the smaller frontier towns implicitly demanded conformity because differences stuck out so vividly. Except for blacks and Indians, by the 1950s and 1960s most foreign-born immigrants had been at least partially, if not completely, assimilated.

However, if a new foreign-born immigrant was distinctly different from the previous immigrant waves, it took them longer to assimilate. For example, during 1910 and 1920 the Eastern Europeans, who came from many different countries, spoke different languages, practiced different religions such as Christian Orthodox, and faced more difficulty "fitting-in."

Swedes, who may have come at the same time as the Eastern Europeans, benefited from the other Swedes who preceded them and had already been accepted by the "mainstream" culture. Generally, the Eastern Europeans found work in the mines and settled primarily near Rock Springs and Sheridan, Wyoming.

Today in Wyoming, the influx of immigrants or "newcomers" continues. For example, from 2007 to 2008, Wyoming's overall population grew by 9,416 (or almost 18%). Of that increase, a mere 40% (or 3,826 people) resulted from more births than deaths. Immigration accounted for 60% (or 5,692 people) of the total population increase. Five percent came from other countries.

Before moving to Wyoming, where did the recent newcomers live? We can determine their state and country of origin by using the U.S. Census Bureau's 2006 American Community Survey, Internal Revenue Service Records of

Saving the Best of the West in Wyoming

Wyoming federal tax returns, and the Wyoming Department of Transportation's driver's licenses exchange data. No matter the measure, they all show a similar pattern.

With respect to states of origin, by far and away the most newcomers came from Colorado (12%) and California (18%). Utah and Montana both account for nearly 8% of domestic immigrants. Although sending fewer than Utah or Montana, New Mexico, Arizona, and South Dakota round out the states that together account for about one-half of Wyoming immigrants. The other 50% of today's Wyoming immigrants come from the rest of the U.S. or a foreign country.

With respect to international immigrants, beginning in 2000 and ending in 2005, two groups dominated immigration. The first group came from Central and South America, and other arrived from Europe and Eastern Europe. Only in 2003, did the total number of international immigrants exceed 2,000, and that was due to an atypically large influx of 1,002 Asians.

It appears that the Wyoming surge of Asians was part of a much larger and more sustained immigration of Asians. The Immigration Act of 1990 increased the number of Asians coming to the U.S by raising the total quota and reorganizing the system of preferences to favor professions such as medicine, technology, investment, and other specialties. It estimated that from 1990 to 2005, 4.5 million skilled Asians had immigrated to the United States.

Further confounding the idea of "native Wyomingites" are the facts that in 2006, the U.S.

Census' American Community Survey shows that only 43% of Wyoming's population was born in the state whereas 59% of all other Americans were born in their state of residence. In contrast to popular perception, Wyoming has been and continues as a state of immigrants, and they have and will continue to enrich and change it.

Only one ethnic and cultural group could potentially bring a much needed technicolor of diversity to Wyoming's current whiteness. Those who are Hispanic or Latino (of any race) deserve more attention. In 2006, 6.9% of Wyoming's total population or 35,732 were Hispanic or Latino. The Hispanic and Latino population has been the fastest growing segment of Wyoming's population, and between 2000 and 2006 it grew 12.8% compared to the 3.1% growth of non-Hispanic whites.

Aside from its growth rate, the Hispanic and Latino population is much younger than Wyoming's total population. Their median age is 25 compared to Wyoming's median age of 36. The Hispanic and Latino's median income is also lower. It is $34,970 compared to Wyoming's median income of $45,685. Of those over 25 years of age, only 28% of the Hispanic and Latino population was foreign-born. That suggests that they are somewhat similar to the other ethnic groups who earlier immigrated to Wyoming. Most Hispanic and Latinos appear to have settled in other states before moving to Wyoming. It is too early to tell whether or not that will speed their assimilation.

Sixty-three percent of Wyoming's Hispanic and Latino population have Mexican ancestry, and 35% have ancestors from Central America. About 60% of Wyoming's Hispanic and Latinos live in four counties—28% in Laramie County, 11.2% in Sweetwater County, 10% in Natrona, and 8% in Albany County.

The Cowboy State

At the very beginning of this book, I used the example of the new Wyoming state quarter to question whether the Equality State or the Cowboy State most accurately captures not only Wyoming's past and present, but its more enduring and unifying spirit. By now the reader knows that the Equality State motto—more myth than reality—is not a truthful answer to the question. In addition, by limiting opportunities and clearly classifying women and minorities as second class citizens, the state's insularity can hurt people's chances in life.

Although the Big Wonderful can have its moments, the Cowboy State and its quintessential bucking horse and rider best represent the essence of Wyoming history, and how it is unfolding today.

By highlighting Wyoming's immigrant and diverse history, this chapter, *Newcomers and Old Timers,* has erased any meaningful distinction between the two. At one time, every resident of Wyoming came from someplace else. But these waves of immigrants, their isolation, and their hardships created the need for a force that could unify them and give them a shared spiritual lift.

In the early days and even today, Wyoming's nearly unreachable skyline and sparse population moved people to search for their identity. They needed to know who they were, what bound them together, what set them apart from the rest of the world, and what was distinctly theirs. But to bring together the old and newer immigrants that identity needed to reach beyond the state's limited cultural and geographic boundaries. They also looked for an identity that would give them strength and have some symmetry with the striking natural world and way of life around them.

Wyoming's answer to the question of its identity became and remains the cowboy. His real and mythical character, horsemanship, marksmanship, freedom, and independence also made him a hero with universal appeal. Further, Wyoming and the West's succeeding waves of new immigrants, who were unrestricted by convention or heredity, symbolized what Wallace Stegner called the "geography of hope." Generation after generation could leave their troubles behind and start anew in the West.

William Sublette, mountain man, explorer, and businessman, brought five head of cattle to the 1830 rendezvous on the Green River. They were the first cattle in Wyoming, but did not stay. Beginning in the 1840s and continuing into the 1860s, thousands of cattle came to Wyoming, but they were just summer guests feeding on the range of southeastern Wyoming and further north in Montana.

Only 8,143 cattle were counted in Wyoming in 1870, yet in a few years ranching would be recognized as the territory's most profitable and sustainable business. According to T.A. Larson's *History of Wyoming*, the September 20, 1875 edition of the *Cheyenne Leader* in conjunction with the *Omaha Herald* listed nineteen Wyoming cattle companies that owned one thousand or more head of cattle. We also know that all three of Wyoming's "Grand Old Men" owned very sizable ranches.

By 1885, cattle herds owned by members of the Wyoming Stock Growers Association had increased to an estimated two million head. Together with the value of real estate, horses, and buildings, the cattle operations were worth $100 million. In today's inflation adjusted terms the estimated value in 1885 equals close to $30 billion.

Even though mining, and most notably coal mining, has played an important role, it never replaced the livestock industry as the defining feature of Wyoming's economy and culture. Even today's 34.4 million acres of privately owned ranchland are home to 1.44 million head of cattle. The average size ranch is 3,780 acres, not including grazing permits on public land, and the annual market value of all Wyoming agricultural products sold approaches $1 billion.

Growing up with the cattle industry was, of course, the cowboy, who at first was not the romantic and near mythical figure we see and imagine today. They were no better and sometimes worse than men in other occupations. For example, our wealthy British friend and rancher, Sir Moreton Frewen, described one of his cowboys in this fashion. "Hank's morals were no doubt primitive, but he was a great flashing gypsy-faced fellow, and I was sorry when having earned two or three hundred dollars, he took the trail again. I hope he is alive and may read this admission of my regard."

Others did not fare so well. T.A Larson in his *History of Wyoming* provides, among others, these two accounts.

"In January 1883, a cowboy named Ed Taylor, otherwise known as Badman Taylor, was shot to death in a Hartville saloon. He was not given a fair chance in a confrontation, but was shot with a rifle through a window. The fact that the previous month Taylor had shot another cowboy in the thigh may have had something to do with his murder."

"In August 1885, while Charley Williams was standing at the bar of a saloon in Lander, Frank Howard placed a revolver near the back of his head

and shot him to death. Formerly gambling partners, they had quarreled."

Writing in the *Classic Cowboy Stories,* Stewart Edward White quoted an old cowboy, who tersely and humorously described life beyond the 100th meridian. The old boy said, *"Son, in this country thar is more cows than butter, more rivers than water, and you kin see farther and see less than any other country in the world."*

Despite these meager, tongue-in-cheek, and sometimes violent beginnings, the cowboy traveled the road to respectability and came to resemble the character we know today. Buffalo Bill's *Wild West Shows*, Owen Wister's *Virginian*, Charlie Russell and Frederick Remington's paintings, dime novels, Saturday morning TV Westerns, and Hollywood movies sped that trip to romantic hero.

Yet just as today's ranching industry is tangible and in many ways similar to cattle ranches in the 1900s, the cowboy is real, too. They still calve, rope, brand, hay, ride round up, and ship their cattle. Beyond machinery, if there is any meaningful difference between now and the old days, it is that the rancher often wears the hat of the cowboy, as well.

There is no denying the near mythical quality of the cowboy. He reaches beyond Wyoming's borders and across our country to the rest of the world. The cowboy carries a legitimacy and longevity that is without parallel. For most residents and non-residents alike, he defines the real appeal of Wyoming. When a symbol or character is so potent, it is not a question of whether it is an accurate portrayal, but rather it is a matter of the character evolving into a reality of its own.

In a way, it is also a state of mind. Thomas Kenneally, who wrote *Schindler's List,* noted "it is not whether a myth is true or not, nor whether it should be true, but that it is somehow truer than truth itself." The cowboy captures the independence and freedom embedded in the human spirit. The vitality and cross-generational appeal of the cowboy rests on his connection to the world that people want to embrace.

In the frontispiece to my book, *Hard and Noble Lives,* I used a quote from Wallace Stegner that best summarized the spirit of my book, the cowboy, and the West. Nothing that I have read since can improve on it.

Western culture and character, hard to define in the first place because they are only half-formed and constantly changing, are further clouded by the mythic stereotype. Why hasn't the stereotype faded away as real cowboys became less and less typical of Western life? Because we can't and won't do without it. But there is the visible pervasive fact of Western space, which acts as a preservative. Space, itself the product of incorrigible aridity and hence more or less permanent, continues to suggest unrestricted freedom, unlimited opportunity for testing and heroisms, a continuing need for self-reliance and physical competence.

Hats off to the Cowboy State!

7

Are the Times
A Changing?

Saving the Best of the West in Wyoming

In many of the earlier chapters I wove together some important features of Wyoming's economic, social and cultural fabric. It is now time to focus more directly on the state's economic and political life, and then determine if the winds of change can blow hard enough to alter the conventional wisdom about Wyoming's economy and politics.

Those conventions first hold that for its entire life, Wyoming's economy has been and will continue to be dependent on cultivating its natural resources whether ranching, coal mining, or drilling for oil and natural gas. As a result, its economy has constantly faced a "boom and bust" cycle.

Next, and despite its early days as a predominately Democratic territory and state, convention contends that for much of its political life Wyoming has been and will continue as a conservative Republican state. While ample evidence can confirm these two conventions, they

159

have almost become articles of faith, thereby obscuring, if not denying, the light breeze of prospective change.

While elected officials and civic leaders can propel change, economic forces will shape the state's politics. For example, big economic forces such as energy development, immigration, very low unemployment rates, and rural sprawl that gobbles up ranchland and open space, can push politics in a more moderate and activist direction. The rise in the number of second homes, residents from other states, environmental threats to a quality environment, and local businesses such as fishing and hunting guides can also lobby for a slower pace of energy development or sustain an amenities-based economy over the longer term.

Economic decline can dramatically change politics, as well.

The Past and Present Economic Life

If the conventional assessment of the past and current structure of Wyoming's economy has one virtue, it would be the simplicity and consistency of the story. From its earliest territorial days through today, its economy has been built on the state's natural resources. The early dominance of the cattle industry and its companion open spaces made Wyoming's economy different than its neighbors'.

Today, that fact preserves more choices about Wyoming's economic future than many recognize. Certainly coal mining and later oil have played more than a supporting role, but the limits imposed by Wyoming's aridity and shortage of water, and the mining industry's relatively small size, stood in contrast to the earlier economies of Colorado and Montana where mining led to their settlement and early growth.

The deep economic and cultural imprint of Wyoming's cattle industry and its ranching tradition emerged during its earliest days. As noted in earlier chapters, in 1870, Wyoming cattle numbered 8,143. By 1878, the number had jumped to close to 300,000 head. The open range and low costs of production made profits possible and, by Wyoming standards, ranching quickly became the state's "big business."

Reflecting its status as Wyoming's most promising economic activity and investment, we already know that by 1885, the state's cattle soared to 1.5 million head and hit a total estimated value of $100 million.

Despite the "killer winter" of 1886-1887 when thousands of cattle perished and foreign investment dropped dramatically, Wyoming's livestock industry has thrived for well over a century. The 650,000 head of cattle in 1893 grew to over 1 million by 1934. In almost every year since 1934, Wyoming's cattle have numbered more than 1 million. In 2005, the state had 1.44 million cattle and they occupied 34.4 million acres. The industry provides 17,000 jobs, and its cattle and calves are now valued at $1.63 billion.

Today when it comes to national rankings, Wyoming's 34.4 million acres of ranch and farm land rank it eighth in the nation. The state's average size ranch or farm of 3,730 acres ranks it "Number One." For the U.S. as a whole, the average size ranch or farm is 444 acres.

This one hundred year stretch of ranching created a strong economic foundation for Wyoming, and it gave rise to the term "cowboy economics" where better livestock management, genetic research, improved productivity, access to capital, and enhanced marketing would lead to continued success.

While cattle ranching found its footing and grew, coal was the step-child of the Union Pacific Railroad. In 1870, 600 Wyoming men mined coal that fired the locomotives of the railroad. By the late 1880s, about 1,000 men mined 1 million tons a year. By comparison, in 1900, West Virginia produced 23 million short tons of coal, and by 1927, West Virginia was producing 146 million tons.

Later in the 20th Century, Wyoming's mineral wealth expanded to include oil, natural gas, trona, and uranium, but the energy industry's alternating booms and busts continued to plague the state. More recently, Wyoming's energy development witnessed a remarkable reversal of fortune. Its abundant coal and natural gas reserves have now proven much larger and more accessible than predicted in the 1980s.

Every year Wyoming produces 440 million tons of coal or almost 39% of the country's coal, and is the nation's number one producer. West Virginia now produces only 13% of the nation's coal. Of course, when coal is burned as a fuel, it emits: carbon dioxide, the main greenhouse gas linked to global warming; sulfur which, when mixed with oxygen, creates acid rain; nitrogen oxide, which can contribute to ozone or smog; and mercury, which can poison fish and other wildlife. Only by solving these environmental problems can Wyoming reach its full potential as a coal producer.

Joining coal, but as a cleaner powerhouse of Wyoming's energy development, is natural gas. Wyoming contains some of the largest natural gas reserves in the lower forty-eight states. The abundance of Wyoming's natural gas reserves places it third in the nation, and its rate of production ranks it second. Its price mirrors its cleanliness and its role as a substitute fuel for high-priced oil. If it can solve some of its own environmental impacts such as ozone, ground water pollution, and threats to prized wildlife habitats and open space, natural gas production and its oil derivative can be a mainstay of Wyoming's economy for another decade or two.

Wyoming's natural gas can give the state breathing space to creatively diversify and magnify its economy. Ranching and the livestock industry gave the state an earlier chance to build a more vibrant and sustainable economy. Today, the ranching industry and an environmentally sound energy industry can unwittingly conspire to give Wyoming a second chance.

To place this historic and contemporary challenge in perspective, let's first take a conventional look at the structure of Wyoming's economy today. Recently, this view, which has been embraced by business leaders, elected officials, and many analysts, has become a self-fulfilling prophecy. Since this perspective requires no leadership, policy decisions, or action, it is also a very comfortable convention.

Whether measured by the percentage of employment or percentage of the state's Gross Domestic Product (GDP), when compared to the U.S. economy, agriculture and mining account for a much larger share of Wyoming's economy. For example, agriculture accounts for 4.1% of Wyoming's employment compared to 2.2% for the nation. Beyond mining and agriculture, construction, the leisure and hospitality industry, and government also account for a larger percentage of jobs in Wyoming than in the country as a whole.

Whether examining Wyoming's GDP, the components of state revenue or its economic growth, the new dominance of the energy industry is striking. It accounts for 30.3% of the state's Gross Domestic Product. The government sector is the next largest at 13.3%. Mineral income composes almost two-thirds of the state's total revenue, and despite price declines in 2008-2009, the longer-term growth of global demand for energy, rising prices, and more development and exploration ensure that Wyoming's growth leader, won't bust for the next decade or two.

For example, in the midst of a deepening 2008 national recession, between July 1, 2007 and July 1, 2008, employment in Wyoming's mining and natural resource sector grew 6.4% —the fastest rate of growth when compared to most other Wyoming industries. Further reflecting the resilience of the energy industry, Wyoming's job growth, low unemployment rates, and per capita income have led most states in the nation.

But with the good comes the bad and maybe

even the ugly. Wyoming's long term dependency on its natural resources, and mining in particular, has also led to the state's distinction as the least diversified economy in the U.S.

The national economy sets the diversification standard at 100%. Missouri almost meets the standard diversification index weighing in at 99.9. All of Wyoming's neighbors, including Utah, Idaho, Colorado, South and North Dakota, Nebraska, and Montana scored 96 and above. Utah sat at the top of the rankings with an index of 99.3, but Idaho, Colorado, and South Dakota were right behind. Even Alaska scored an 85.7. Wyoming occupied the cellar at a stunning 34.9, and that number also set another record in 2006 as the lowest in Wyoming history. That means that Wyoming is becoming dangerously monolithic as an economy and subject to the vagaries of a single and volatile market.

Underscoring that danger is the fact that when mining employment rises, Wyoming's diversification index precipitously declines, and when mining employment declines, the state's diversification index jumps to over 65—still by far the lowest in the country. When mining employment grows, it becomes a larger part of total employment and GDP.

On the surface, this may seem logical. But consider that Wyoming's perennial affliction is its natural resource dependency and the boom and bust economic cycle created by that dependency. When the state has a growing economy, low unemployment rates, and big jumps in county and state revenue, doesn't it make more sense to then invest in new business, attract venture capital, give new business tax breaks, increase support for business incubators, and improve education, apprenticeships, and other high skill job recruitment and training programs?

Today, as in the past, the state tries to increase its economic diversity in an environment of slower growth, much less revenue, rising unemployment, and a drop in business investment—a poor and counterproductive time to try to create new businesses, attract new skilled workers or retain Wyoming's younger workers.

The Future:
Planning for the End
of Roughneck Economics

Although it is now often stated by government and industry officials that this energy boom is not like the short-lived ones of our fathers' or grandfathers' era, this one will end, too. Even though a number of wells may still be producing, when the rigs come down, employment, state and local revenue, and earnings will also come down. The LaBarge and Big Piney fields southwest of Pinedale, where most of the drilling is completed (and some wells depleted), gives us a glimpse of our future.

For example, today almost 43% of Wyoming's natural gas production comes from Sublette

County and its two main fields, the Jonah Field and the Pinedale Anticline. Based on estimates of the Wyoming Oil and Natural Gas Conservation Commission, Jonah Field drilling will be completed in ten more years, and the drilling on the Anticline will last for fifteen. Another 30,000 of about 50,000 coal-bed methane wells in the Powder River Basin will be completed in the next five years. Only one proposed production center in Wamsutter could keep drilling for another twenty to thirty years.

If energy prices stabilize at lower levels and current pipeline capacity does not increase, the number of producing wells may decline even faster. In other words, the state, counties, the energy industry, and businesses have at best ten to fifteen years to invest and build a more diverse and secure economy. Considering the time involved in the planning, design, investment, and management of a more diverse economy, this time frame is very short. Unlike the past, when the modest efforts to diversify the state's economy were launched during economic declines, when the economy is growing is the time to initiate change and invest.

So in what "new" directions can we drive the Wyoming economy, and how can we accelerate the shift to a more diverse and sustainable economic life? Fortunately, the building blocks are already in place, and ironically those blocks take the form of the state's natural resources, including its ranches, open space, bluebird colored sky, clean cool water, and crystal clear air. Energy will also play an important role.

Saving the Best of the West in Wyoming

During the next decade, state government, the University of Wyoming, and the energy industry should collaborate to bring additional value, stability, and environmental friendship to Wyoming's energy resources. The early 2008 agreement between GE Energy and the University of Wyoming offers a near perfect example of this future. That initial agreement and final development agreement reached in late October 2008, enables researchers to develop advanced coal gasification technology for Wyoming's higher moisture sub-bituminous coal. The High Plains Gasification Advanced Technology Center can mark the beginning of a longer-term relationship between Wyoming and GE Energy.

As a leader in cleaner coal integrated gasification, GE Energy has developed a commercially successful process that dramatically reduces carbon dioxide, nitrogen oxide, mercury, and particulates. By extracting gas from coal, the process also uses 30% less water than a pulverized coal plant and can significantly lower transportation costs. Together with more research and development on Wyoming's biological and economic suitability for carbon capture and sequestration, clean coal technology can create a productive, valuable, and environmentally acceptable industry for decades to come.

The recent U.S Department of Energy's $67 million award to the Big Sky Regional Carbon Sequestration Partnership will support a large scale test project that will store more than 2 million tons of carbon dioxide underground in western Wyoming. The eight year project will drill carbon dioxide injection wells about 11,000 feet deep into the Nugget Sandstone formation. According to the Department of Energy, similar sandstone formations can be found throughout the region and could store up to 100 years of carbon dioxide emissions. However, the test project should also determine the pitfalls and environmental consequences of such injection wells.

The inability of the U.S. to find adequate, safe, and acceptable storage for nuclear waste and the indiscriminate discharge of billions of gallons of high salinity water from coal-bed methane wells in Wyoming's Powder River Basin are reminders that caution should not be "thrown to the wind."

Additional cooperative agreements can expand Wyoming's renewable energy resources such as wind and solar. For example, Wyoming is a prime market for wind energy, and wind energy is an industry that is forecast to grow dramatically by 2030. Wyoming currently produces 349.35 megawatts of power through its commercial wind turbines, enough to generate electricity for the equivalent of 87,500 households or about 40% of Wyoming households.

In terms of wind energy potential, Wyoming is ranked seventh in the nation, and it could generate 85,200 megawatts of power and produce 747 billion kilowatts of electricity each year.

By comparison, wind power currently accounts for 48 billion kilowatt hours of electricity a year in the United States—enough to serve 4.5 million households. That is still only about 1% of current demand, but the potential is huge.

By 2030, the U.S. Department of Energy reports that 20% of America's electricity can come from wind. The Great Plains states are home to the greatest wind energy potential in the world. The United States is the "Saudi Arabia" of wind power. When the U.S. is importing nearly 70% of our oil today (compared to 24% in 1970), and when oil prices inevitably rise again, we will send $700 billion or more out of our country every year. Our state needs to take advantage of the winds of change.

Today, the state and its energy companies are now almost rushing to harness Wyoming's wind power potential. In 2008, new turbines built in Converse, Carbon, and Uinta Counties will add 500 more megawatts of wind energy, and that amount is in addition to proposed Power Company of Wyoming's 2,000 megawatt Chokecherry and Sierra Madre Wind Energy Project southeast of Rawlins, Wyoming.

More recently, Anschutz Power Company of Wyoming has proposed installing an additional 2,000 megawatts of wind generation in Carbon County. It joined Rocky Mountain Power, who plans to add 3,000 megawatts of wind power. Anschutz will also build a $3 billion, 900 mile long high voltage power line that will serve the Desert Southwest.

However, the scale and siting of the big commercial turbines must recognize the potential adverse impacts on wildlife, archaeological sites, and preservation of historical places.

Not only can wind power provide megawatts of electricity to serve many customers, but small wind power projects can provide electricity for ranchers and smaller communities. GE Energy is also one of the world's largest manufacturers of wind turbines, and this seems to create another opportunity for collaboration.

Similarly, Wyoming and its energy industry should take advantage of GE Energy's ecomagination program. That program certifies numerous company products as means to market technologies that can help customers meet pressing environmental challenges.

For example, GE Energy has developed an Integrated Compressor Line for the oil and gas industry that is driven by high speed electric motors and can reduce carbon dioxide emissions by 1,520 tons a year and cut the use of lubricant oil by 38,250 liters. As a $22 billion company, GE Energy must be doing something right.

The future cost of oil and its fragile supply ensures that in the future all of these technologies, including clean coal, could gain substantial cost and efficiency advantages.

A second economic diversification initiative that would engage the state government and the energy industry is the formation of a sizable Wyoming Venture Capital Fund. The Fund can underwrite new businesses and technology based in Wyoming or new ventures whose research or products can directly benefit the Wyoming economy. As long as the energy industry continues to handsomely profit from Wyoming's natural gas, oil, and coal, it should help ensure a more viable and diverse economy. Those investments can serve as a hedge against the day when the energy industry inevitably downsizes.

As part of some of the agreements to drill on public lands, the energy industry already provides multi-million dollar funds to help mitigate its adverse environmental effects. This venture capital fund extends the mandated mitigation to the socio-economic realm and will lead to a more vibrant and sustainable economy.

Third, the energy industry, the state, the University of Wyoming, and local communities should collaborate to start a few well funded and designed business incubators that help new start-up businesses. Some may even benefit from the Venture Capital Fund.

They should provide space, seed capital, technical assistance, financial management expertise, a potential pool of employees and a human resource guide. These incubators need real resources including money, technical support, and business plan development. Each can focus on a specific business such as engineering, medical services or architecture, and these initial few incubators can serve as pilot programs that can test the incubators' success rate over a five year time period and make adjustments when necessary.

The Venture Capital Fund and the business incubators can be complemented with investment and wage tax credits for new businesses and innovation centers providing new ideas and technology for start-ups.

While better job training and post-secondary

education can also improve Wyoming's economy and help retain the eighteen to twenty-four year olds—who still leave the state in droves—it is now time to shift to Wyoming's new economic direction: Cowboy Economics Redux, that fundamentally combines a reignited ranching industry with property income, cultural and traditional tourism, and professional and business services where the natural environment is exploited as a place rather than exclusively as source of raw materials.

The logic of this combination will soon become apparent, but the lead actors in this play will also need a best supporting actress, and in this case she is Wyoming's *professional, scientific, and technical services. Retail trade* will also play more than a cameo role. But let's first start with the defining features of Cowboy Economics Redux.

We have already taken a conventional look at the composition of the state's Gross Domestic Product and those sectors that account for much of the state's employment. We have also compared theses numbers to the U.S. economy as a whole. No matter the more traditional perspectives, the state's continued dependency on its natural resources has almost become an article of faith.

However, a more accurate and revisionist view of the state's economic structure and opportunities has emerged from an analysis of personal income or the source of Wyoming workers' earnings by industry. Of course, jobs or employment are important, and so is the larger, yet more abstract, Gross Domestic Product. But the best measure of our residents' economic well-being is their personal income and the source of that income. The earnings data can also better reveal the sectors that increasingly account for larger shares of income and our best bets for the future.

In 2007, and according to the most recent data from the U.S. Department of Commerce's Bureau of Economic Analysis, Wyoming's total personal income stood at $24,617,609,000 or almost $25 billion. Five years earlier it was $15.5 billion. It grew close to 60% over five years. In 2007, per capita personal income was $47,047 compared to $31,115 in 2002.

However, the most dramatic part of this story is the amount of personal earnings that comes from "non-labor income" which includes dividends, interest, rent and retirement. In 2007, income from dividends, interest, and rent was $7,241,660,000 or well over $7 billion. Retirement income totaled $2,656,837,000. Combined, in 2007, dividends, interest, rent and retirement equaled $9,898,497,000 or around $10 billion. That accounts for 40% of Wyoming's total personal income.

In short, this is "investment income" or "property income." Its sources are residents with high incomes, retirees, residents who saved and invested, and those who relocated to Wyoming for the state's natural beauty and other amenities. Often those residents who have relocated, are known as "amenities immigrants." This income is circulated when it is spent on the purchase of goods and services. It also can stabilize an economy when traditional wages and employment decline.

This $10 billion in non-labor income has grown from $2.7 billion in 1990. For purposes of comparison today, in 2007, the mining sector accounted for $3.1 billion in earnings or just 12.5% of total personal income. Even civilian government—the federal, state, and local government combined—generated over $3.7 billion in earnings.

The growth of personal income and the very dominant role of non-labor income is a long term trend. Beginning in 1998, each year has shown steady and substantial growth in personal income and the non-labor component of it. Although data is limited for 2008, it shows a continuation of that trend. For example, personal income jumped by close to $2 billion and the yield from dividends, interest, and rents rose by 5.2%.

Let's take a look at another amenities based industry, *travel and tourism*. According to a very detailed economic study of the industry by Dean Runyan and Associates in 2006, travel accounted for $2.5 billion in direct spending. That has grown from $1.4 billion in 1997, or by an annual average growth rate of 6.4%.

Wyoming residents account for $532 million in annual travel and tourism spending, and those from other states account for $1.9 billion in direct spending. Foreign visitors account for the remainder. But for the purpose of a more direct comparison, the *travel and tourism industry*

Saving the Best of the West in Wyoming

accounted for $624 million in earnings or 3% of the state's total earnings.

The Wyoming tourism industry is a mix of "ma and pa" businesses, world class resorts, dude ranches, and wide open spaces anchored by the gems of Yellowstone and Teton National Parks. In 2007, 3,151,343 people visited Yellowstone National Park, and another 2,588,574 visited Grand Teton National Park. That same year saw an additional 322,273 visit Devil's Tower, Wyoming's third most popular recreation site.

When the earnings for travel and tourism are added to the current amenities based economy, it totals $10.5 billion or 43% of the state's total personal income and that does not include another $2.7 billion in transfer payments, including those eligible for disability.

Aside from Yellowstone and Teton National Parks that in 2007 accounted for 2.1% of all national park visits in the U.S., ranches are the real anchors of both the traditional economy and the new economy that is based on recreation, natural amenities, and cultural tourism. These economic magnets not only retain and attract people for outdoor experiences such as fishing and hiking, but draw them closer with historic landmarks, art galleries, theater, music, furniture, Western antiques, and other Western collectibles.

Of course, the national forests and other public lands support this new economy, but whether it is open space, big vistas, wildlife, rivers, streams, grassland, and even the cultural appeal of the Cowboy State, ranches hold the keys to the doors of the future.

Over a decade of research and data gathering by the U.S. Department of Agriculture's Economic Research Service dramatically shows that the fastest rate of economic and population growth of non-metro America or its rural counties is tied directly to the amenities offered by smaller or mid-sized towns in the Rocky Mountain West, including Wyoming. Those amenities include recreation, open space, national parks and forests, a variety of stores, restaurants, and good medical care.

Wyoming could benefit from more frequent public opinion surveys that can gauge the "state of the state" or broader views on the direction of the state, including agriculture, tourism, energy development, housing, open space, clean air and water, and politics. Currently, most state polls concentrate on a single issue such as a smoking ban or a sales tax exemption for food. However, a few in-depth polls on important issues have been fielded.

For example, in 2007, a statewide poll on natural resource conservation and development was sponsored by the University of Wyoming's Ruckelshaus Institute of Environment and Natural Resources, the Wyoming Stock Growers Association, and the Wyoming Chapter of the Nature Conservancy. The three top concerns of the 600 randomly selected registered voters were:

1) the availability of water for farming and ranching (57%)

2) loss of family farms and ranches (47%)

Saving the Best of the West in Wyoming

3) the natural areas and ranch lands being split up by new housing development (44%)

With respect to state support for conservation priorities the sample selected the following top five projects:

1) keeping and storing more Wyoming water in the state (86%)

2) maintaining the strength of Wyoming's agriculture and tourism industries (77 %)

3) preserving open spaces and scenic vistas (70%)

4) protecting the water quality of rivers, lakes, and streams (70%)

5) preserving the family farm (67%)

More recently in May, 2009, and as part of a statewide initiative known as Building the Wyoming We Want, a firm, Hart + Mind Strategies, conducted a poll of 894 members of the general public, who live in Wyoming and were eighteen years old or older.
When asked if they thought that *protecting land and water* was more important than *development and economic growth,* 54% picked *protecting land and water* and 37% chose *economic growth and development.*

In this sample, 72% of the public "believes that farming and ranching are critical to the future of Wyoming and help maintain the land, open spaces, wildlife, and values that are so important to making Wyoming a great place to live."

When asked to think about agriculture and ranching and the role they play in the state of Wyoming, what value, if any, do you believe they bring to their communities, 57% said *a great deal of value* and 34% *a fair amount of value* and 91% ascribed real value to agriculture and ranching.

Wyoming citizens not only see the importance of ranching but clearly see the connection between ranching, open spaces, water quality, and tourism—all are very highly valued, and their preservation is seen as central to the state's future. But today the economic survival of many ranches and ranchers is far from certain. Rising costs and volatile markets make ranching less and less profitable—never a get rich quick way of life.

Some ranches or parts of them have been sold for residential and commercial development. The average age of the Wyoming rancher is 54.1 years old, and that means many ranches will change hands in the next ten years. The state and counties must become more active in preserving ranches or risk their last chance to build a sustainable and more diverse economy. Also, if the energy industry does not clean up its environmental act, the air and water pollution will also deter a transition to a better economic future. An area's reputation for greenhouse gas emissions and ozone will certainly limit its appeal to tourists, fishermen, hunters, investors, new businesses, and amenity immigrants.

The tangible need for a more thoughtful and activist strategy for ranchland preservation can be found in the county where my family lives, Sublette County. During the early months of 2008, the current owners of two historic ranches along the Green River agreed to place around nineteen thousand acres of their ranches under conservation easements and allow the Wyoming Game and Fish to manage public access to a 4.5 mile long stretch of the Green River. They do not want to subdivide their ranches and would like to preserve some historic ranch houses and other buildings.

This is an unprecedented offer. However, they need millions in compensation for this land and an agreement to at least let the current generation ranch until they retire. Rather than the county commission, governor, large dollar donors to environmental causes, and the energy industry initially taking the lead, these ranchers have been scrambling to raise the money, and today they candidly say that it is a long shot.

As noted in the chapter, *Odds and Ends,* the energy industry in the form of Jonah Interagency Office stepped up and committed the first $5 million of about a $20 million project. Just after that commitment, the state's Wildlife and Natural Resources Trust broke with its tradition and committed another $1.2 million for this project. Both boosted the prospect of preserving these ranches.

When the energy industry booms again in Sublette County, we will need to preserve some of our best ranches or we will lose our heritage and chance to sustain our appeal and growth.

But let's look at the "sunny side of life" and assume that ranching and a new interpretation of cowboy economics will prevail. Why not?

A detailed 2007 study, *The Changing Structure of Montana's Economy* by Kara Grau at the University of Montana showed that Montana has already made the transition to a recreation and tourism based economy, and that transition has not resulted in a steep decline in wages. For example, in Montana from 1994 to 2004 the service sector's earnings kept pace with the natural resource industry earnings.

Just like the "old" economy, the new one will rely on ranching. The major players in Wyoming's new economy are ranchers, retirees, traditional tourists, cultural tourists, investors, property owners, amenity immigrants, and technical support such as telecommunications, finance, insurance, and computers that make all of those earnings possible. But the long-run success of the new economy requires the support of a few strong and compatible industries. The primary candidate for best supporting role is *professional and technical services. Retail trade* turns in a strong performance, as well.

Before a more detailed preview of those sectors, two other features of Wyoming's economy should be mentioned. First, construction accounts

Saving the Best of the West in Wyoming

for $1.66 billion in earnings or 6.7% of total personal income. Measured by earnings, it is the fifth largest industry in Wyoming. Some of that construction is tied to the energy industry and other large commercial projects, but construction, including homebuilding and the timber industry, is a victim of the same boom and bust cycle our new economy will try to minimize.

Second, we know when compared to the U.S. economy, Wyoming's share of employment or Gross Domestic Product accounted for by *professional and business services* is 4.2% of GDP compared to 11.8% for the nation as a whole.

Wyoming need not strive to look like the U.S. economy. In fact, no matter how hard we might try, the state would not succeed in mirroring the national economy. Instead, our goal should be to look at our own economy and make judgments about the sectors that have the greatest promise and can help lead us to a more diverse and sustainable future.

Professional, scientific, and technical services encompasses management companies, support services and administrative services, and waste management and remediation firms. In 2007, the industry totaled $775,892,000 in earnings or 3.2% of the state's total earnings. These professions tend to represent what many consider the "better and higher wage" jobs. In 2002, this industry contributed $519,779,000 to the state's earnings, and between 2002 and 2007, earnings in the professional, scientific, and technical services industry grew by 50%. If we added professions and industries very similar to the *professional, scientific, and technical services* sector, including *information* such as the Internet, broadcasting and telecommunications; *finance and insurance* such as banks, insurance, and securities; and *real estate*, including rentals and leasing, in 2007, together all of these professions or industries accounted for $1.88 billion in state earnings or 7.6% of total earnings. This earnings profile places these industries fourth on the state's income hit parade—behind non-labor income, government, and mining.

The decision to build the $80 million National Center for Atmospheric Research's supercomputer near Cheyenne, Wyoming, testifies to the growth potential and stability of this new combination of professional services. This supercomputer will be one of the world's most powerful computers and dedicated to a better scientific understanding of climate change, severe weather, and air quality. The center will also house a premier data storage and archival facility that will hold an irreplaceable history of climate records.

Not only does this new combination of professional services represent a thriving industry in its own right, but it also provides the professional and technical support for ranchers, other property owners, traditional tourists, cultural and heritage tourists, investors, and amenity immigrants whose business interests and activity make up Wyoming's new economy. As these professional services have no adverse impact on the environment, they are even more in sync with the new economy.

The last important performer for the new

economy is *retail trade* which includes motor vehicle and parts dealers, furniture and home furnishings, electronics and appliance stores, building material and garden supply stores, food and beverage stores, health and personal care stores, gas stations, clothing and clothing accessories stores, sporting goods, hobby, book and music stores, general merchandise stores, miscellaneous store retailers, and nonstore retailers. These businesses account for $1,024,769,000 in state earnings or 4.2% of total earnings. That amount ranks it sixth when compared to all other industries.

Similar to the expanded *professional services sector*, any population will find this array of retail stores essential for daily living, but the demand from members of the new economy will also support these services. Again, the retail industry's environmental footprint is very small and poses no threat to open space, wildlife habitat, clear air, and clean water so central to Wyoming's future appeal and the growth of the retail sector.

The three pillars of Wyoming's future—non-labor income, broadly defined professional and technical services, and retail trade contribute almost $13.5 billion in income or 55% of Wyoming's total earnings.

As we begin building a new foundation for Wyoming's economy, oddly enough we can learn from Saudi Arabia, the king of oil and oil reserves. For example, the Saudis hold at least 25% of the world's known oil reserves. In the last two years alone, they reported oil income of $700 billion. Despite its oil riches that will last for decades, the Saudis are looking beyond oil and building new cities and a new economy.

According to Faiza Saleh Ambah of the *Washington Post* Foreign Service, Saudi officials are spending billions of dollars to transform the desert around Medina into a "buzzing hub of scientific research and development, with cutting edge universities, hospitals, and housing for more than 130,000 people attracted by the idea of living in the city where Islam's prophet, Muhammad, is buried."

In the July 21-27, 2008 *Weekly Edition of the Washington Post*, Faiza Saleh Ambah continues, "The project called the Knowledge Economic City represents the first serious step by Saudi Arabia toward building a post-petroleum economy."

The new city near Medina is one of six new major industrial centers to rise over the next fifteen years. They have committed at least $100 billion to their new economy. Expecting a push to alternative fuels, a former Saudi oil minister wryly observed, "the Stone Age did not end for lack of stone."

My assessment of Wyoming's economic past, present, and future began with a conventional analysis of Wyoming's dangerous economic dependency on its natural resources, particularly mining, and the boom and bust cycle that accompanies this dependency. I have offered proposals for a transition to a more diverse and sustainable economy. They include cleaner coal, cleaner production of natural gas, a sizable future in wind energy, a venture capital fund to help underwrite new and innovative businesses, and finally the linchpin of our economy's past, present, and future, ranching.

My review of the state's economic future highlighted the end of "roughneck" economics and the beginning of Cowboy Economics Redux. The magnet for the new economy is the ranching industry, its open space, big vistas, wildlife, cultural appeal and other amenities. Together they retain or attract wealth, tourism, cultural tourists, and amenity immigrants.

It is now time for the curtain call that will close this section on Wyoming's economy. When it comes to the state's economic life, the "times really are a changing." Some forces are already in play that will alter the state's economic structure. The state, the energy industry, and others can take actions that will further diversify and strengthen Wyoming's future.

The three forces that will shape the future are:

1) the overwhelmingly dominant role of non-labor income in the state's economy

2) the appeal of prospectively vibrant professional, technical service, financial, and real estate industries

3) the foundation of a stable retail industry

Clean energy, wind power, venture capital, and a strongly supported ranching industry will finally lead the way to a more stable, richer, and better life or "heaven on Wyoming earth."

Wyoming Politics: Entering the 21st Century

Just as most of the conventional stories about Wyoming's economy were simple and consistent, the past and present beliefs about the state's politics are simple, as well. They hold that Wyoming has been and remains a conservative Republican state. While many Wyoming voters claim that they vote for the man (or woman) and not the political party, whether measured by registration or voting performance Wyoming is overwhelmingly Republican. Although some important exceptions will emerge, Wyoming has been a very "red" state.

For example, on Election Day, November 4, 2008, of the 244,818 registered voters, 27% were

Democrats (65,640); not even .5% were
Libertarians (878); 62% were Republicans
(150,504); and 11% were Independents (27,757).
Registered Wyoming Republicans out-numbered
registered Democrats 2.3 to 1.

In 2009, there were 41 Republicans and
19 Democrats in the Wyoming House of
Representatives. The Wyoming Senate had 23
Republicans and 7 Democrats.

In the 2008 Presidential campaign,
McCain/Palin received 164,958 (or 2,671 fewer
votes than Bush/Cheney received in 2004),
and Obama/Biden garnered 82,868 votes (or
12,002 more votes than Kerry/Edwards received
in 2004). These vote totals translate into
64% of the vote for McCain/Palin and 32% for
Obama/Biden. Due to a surge in same-day
registration, over 11,000 more voted than had
been registered earlier that day. It appears that
Obama/Biden were the primary beneficiaries of
that surge.

Both of Wyoming's U.S. Senators are
Republicans and were elected in 2008 by wide
margins over their Democratic opponents. In
fact, both senators received about 20,000 more
votes than McCain/Palin. The lone Wyoming
member of the U.S. House of Representatives,
a Republican, retired at the end of 2008, and
another Republican, Cynthia Lummis, handily,
but surprisingly, defeated Democrat, Gary
Trauner, for the open seat. She won by 52.7%
to 42.8%.

On a brighter note for Wyoming Democrats,
they have held the governor's mansion for

twenty-four out of the last thirty-two years. Also, it appears that in 2004, 2006, and even 2008, that Democrats were increasingly competitive for the state's single member U.S. House District.

For example, in 2004, Ted Ladd, the Democrat, lost to then incumbent, Barbara Cubin, by 55% to 42%. But Ladd picked up almost 33,000 more votes than the Democratic candidate in 2002. In a similar vein, Gary Trauner barely lost to Republican incumbent, Barbara Cubin, in 2006. Trauner received 92,324 votes versus Cubin's 93,336—a razor thin margin of about one vote per precinct. Incidentally, in a losing race in 2008, Trauner still received 106,758 votes— 14,434 more votes than he earned in 2006 and almost 40% of his vote came from Independents or Republicans.

The lower turn-out in 2006 and the closer race may have been partially driven by an anti-Cubin vote among independent voters, and some Republicans may have just stayed home.

Although these developments may presage some modest shift in favor of Democrats or Independents, any meaningful breath of change must have its origins deeper in the minds of voters. First, we know that the state is witnessing significant economic and social change, and political change may follow. The overwhelming role of non-labor income in the state's economic structure means that the numbers of amenity immigrants, retirees, semi-retirees, property owners, and cultural tourists are growing. They possess the potential to shift the state's politics, and in some cities and counties they already have changed local politics.

To underscore this growing power, in Teton County between 2004 and 2008, Republicans dropped from 50% of registered voters to 42.9% whereas Democrats jumped from 23% of registered voters to 33%. Independents accounted for 23% of registered voters and hold the balance of electoral power.

Even more telling are the actual votes. In 2008, Teton County voted overwhelmingly for Obama/Biden, who captured 61% of the vote. That means that 28% of the Obama/Biden vote came from Independents or Republicans.

Today, in my county, Sublette County, has 2,973 registered Republicans, 457 registered Democrats, and 342 Independents. Compared to 2004, registered Republicans dropped by 10%. Democrats increased by 10% and Independents grew by 60%.

While the county is still overwhelmingly Republican, in 2008, it did help elect, Jim Roscoe, a Democrat, to the county's statehouse legislative seat, House District 22. He replaced a Republican.

We also know from the chapter, *Newcomers and Old Timers,* that only 40% of the state's population are native Wyomingites or born in the state where they now live. Six in ten came from another state or country. We also know that most of Wyoming's recent and remarkable population growth was due to immigration, not from substantially more births than deaths and that many of the new immigrants came from states such as Colorado or California, with strong Democratic traditions.

Saving the Best of the West in Wyoming

If economic and demographic changes are harbingers of political change, where can we find the seeds of that change? The best places to see if the seeds have germinated are the two most recent very competitive statewide elections.

The first election is Governor Dave Freudenthal's inaugural run for governor in 2002. His opponent was Republican candidate, Eli Bebout, and a Libertarian candidate also ran. Freudenthal won with 49.96% of the vote and Bebout gained 47.92%. Dawson, the Libertarian, received 3,924 votes or 2%. Turnout was 185,459 or well over 80% of registered voters.

The other race is the 2006 contest between Democrat Gary Trauner, and Republican incumbent, Barbara Cubin. In a relatively high turnout election, Cubin beat Trauner by 50.3% to 49.7%. Even though Trauner lost in 2008, these two elections can tell us from what counties competitive Democrats are drawing most of their votes and where they are beginning to gain additional votes. When compared to 2006, Trauner's 2008 loss can also pinpoint in what crucial counties he failed to keep his 2006 margins or lost to Lummis.

Competitive Democrats draw most of their votes from the larger population centers. They won handily in Albany County, Carbon County, Laramie County, and Natrona County. Democrats also gained strength in Sweetwater County, and Teton County. Fifty percent of the state's residents lived in these six counties.

A table showing the Democrats' margins in these two elections can be found in the *Appendix*.

In 2008, not only was Cynthia Lummis much more competitive in Albany and Laramie Counties, but she beat Gary Trauner in Carbon and Natrona Counties. Only in Sweetwater and Teton Counties did Trauner match his 2006 margins.

The counties where Democrats are increasingly competitive are Converse, Fremont, Hot Springs, Platte, and Sheridan Counties. Again, the vote totals for our two races can be found in the *Appendix*. These five counties account for another 18% of the state's population. Together all eleven of these counties account for 68% of the state's population and most of its voters.

Some analysts might point out that in the 2002 gubernatorial election, Bebout was handicapped by the fact that Republican, Jim Geringer, had just completed two terms or eight years in Wyoming's governor's mansion. Bebout was further injured by a mounting financial scandal. As already mentioned, Trauner's appeal in 2006 may have been as much an anti-Cubin vote as a vote for Trauner. It is also possible that a number of Independents and moderate Republicans, who voted for Obama, felt that further "down ticket" they needed to restore their Republican credentials.

Nevertheless, the conventional view that Wyoming is a solid and unimpeachably Republican state can't explain why these races were so competitive. Some counties, such as Albany, Carbon, Laramie, and Natrona gave both Freudenthal and Trauner very big margins. Some of them reported registration numbers that favored Republicans and often by a hefty amount.

Saving the Best of the West in Wyoming

For example, Natrona County has twice as many registered Republicans as Democrats, yet voted overwhelmingly for Freudenthal and Trauner.

Political change in Wyoming has typically run at a very slow pace, and if a more moderate and independent electorate can cross the finish line, it will depend on a broad change in attitudes as well. Economic and demographic changes contribute to attitudinal change, but we need to look more directly at the attitudes themselves. Unfortunately, few polls of Wyoming voters or residents can let us handicap the speed of a shift, if any.

Although Wyoming's brand of conservatism may have some unique features such as relishing its tradition of rugged independence, on a fundamental level it embraces the same conservative tenets as other Americans. In decades of opinion research and regardless of political party identification, when asked whether "the federal government does too many things that people can do better for themselves," people tend to say that it does too many things (45%) or struck the right balance (21%). Only 23% said that the federal government should do more.

Similarly, when asked if "the federal government has the right amount of power, too much, or not enough," 46% of Americans say that it has about the right amount of power; 42% say too much; and a mere 7% believe it does not have enough.

But that same opinion research tells another

and near opposite story about voters. When asked about government in *general,* people tend to be *ideological conservatives.* But when asked about the *specific things* government actually does, they emerge as *operational liberals.*

For example, 72% want to increase federal funding for medical research, and another 27% want to keep it at current levels; and 61% want to increase federal funding for teachers' salaries in poor school districts with another 26% saying that it should stay at present levels.

Since 1964 and through today, social scientists and opinion researchers have consistently found this paradox among the American public. Although more and better research on Wyoming public opinion may reveal some differences from national public opinion, it is unlikely that Wyoming residents will fundamentally differ on the nation's paradox or ambivalence about the federal government.

This likely ambivalence about government among Wyoming's Republicans can first be seen in their support for state and local governments. Whether measured as a percentage of employment or Gross Domestic Product, they are larger than the federal government. First, 56,447 individuals work for Wyoming's state or local governments. No other industry in Wyoming employs that many people. By comparison, retail trade employs 41,691, construction 36,660, and mining only 31,009 people. In Wyoming, government accounts for 14.5% of all employment compared to 13.7%

for the U.S. In addition, government accounts for 13.3% of Wyoming's Gross Domestic Product compared to 11.9% for the United States.

Perhaps, the most striking number is the $2.655 billion in personal earnings generated by state and local government employment. When it comes to personal income, state and local government takes a bronze medal as the third largest industry in Wyoming.

Clearly, Wyoming citizens and elected officials support a large and growing government that provides critical services to people.

The 2007 public opinion poll on natural resource conservation and development showed similar predispositions towards operational liberalism. Seventy-four percent supported "setting aside more state money to protect land, air, water, wildlife and ranch lands." This idea was strongly favored by 37%. Funding Wyoming's Wildlife and Natural Resource Trust to $200 million by 2010 was favored by 69%. Even more surprisingly, 55% of the poll's respondents supported an increase in local taxes to "obtain state matching funds to protect water, wildlife habitat, and ranch lands in their communities, and 74% favored impact fees on developers who build in areas where development may adversely affect water, wildlife, and working ranches.

The analysis earlier in this chapter suggested that the winds of economic change are strong enough to alter the state's longstanding dependency, exploitation, and consumption of its natural resources. In conjunction with the energy industry, counties, and the University of Wyoming, the state can accelerate that shift to Cowboy Economics Redux and help bring to fruition a more vibrant and sustainable economy. This strategy is the road to the preservation of "what makes Wyoming, Wyoming."

New residents and new values will also change the state's politics. At the presidential level, Wyoming will certainly retain its status as a very red state for some time. But the breeze of political change has picked up. The breeze is not yet strong enough to blow in anything resembling realignment to a competitive two party state. But the growth of Independents could hold the balance of power in future elections.

Most importantly, Democrats, Independents, and Republicans will have to earn an improved political standing with the electorate by building a new and stronger economy and preserving Wyoming's clear air, clean water, its big vistas, wildlife, and ranchland. All define its economic future. Whoever wins this campaign for a new economy will eventually succeed at the polls.

Saving the Best of the West in Wyoming

8

A Survivor's Guide for Living in the West

Saving the Best of the West in Wyoming

The first American survivalists in the West, who honed their skills over centuries, were the American Indians. Walking in their footsteps were Lewis and Clark and the Corps of Discovery, the first white men to explore and open the West. Their well-documented journey of survival was heroic and historic. The second transcontinental story of survival and adventure is underappreciated compared to the Corps of Discovery.

In 1811, five years after the conclusion of the Lewis and Clark expedition, Wilson Price Hunt and his party, who worked for John Jacob Astor, crossed the continent when traveling west to Astoria, Oregon. In 1812, his colleague, Robert Stuart, who initially sailed to Astoria, returned East by the overland route and was the third explorer to complete the transcontinental trip.

The mountain men, who spanned a single generation, represented the epitome of the wilderness survivors, and they had none of today's camping conveniences such as down sleeping bags, high tech tents, battery powered lights, GPS, and Coleman stoves. However, those early survivalists were few in number.

Surviving the Oregon Trail

The first "great migration" West followed the two thousand mile Oregon Trail. For twenty-five years from 1843 until 1869 when the transcontinental railroad was completed, more than 500,000 immigrants from the East and Midwest traveled the Oregon-California Trail to Oregon, Washington, California, Nevada, Idaho, and Utah. It was the only practical corridor to the Western United States. The overland trip to Oregon took four to six months and sometimes longer.

Until the construction of the Oregon Short Line in the early 1880s which connected Granger, Wyoming, to Portland, Oregon, the later emigrants and stockmen still used the trail, but just not as many traveled it as in the earlier years.

From many diaries, "emigrant" guides, and histories, we know that the journey west was extremely difficult for all travelers and fatal for many. One in ten died on the trail, and a total of thirty-four thousand perished. Many had to walk the whole distance and some barefoot. If an emigrant family ran out of flour on the journey, the purchase price of $4 per barrel at the beginning of the trip rose to $1 per pint. Coffee on the trail also cost $1 per pint. The real threats to trail life were inadequate preparation, insufficient supplies, cholera, poor sanitation, and accidental gunshot wounds. The Indians were generally more helpful than harmful.

These hardships and stories can provide us with the first survivor's guide for immigrants moving west. Even though a different time in history, the Oregon Trail survivors' guides such as Lansford W. Hastings' 1845 *Emigrants' Guide to Oregon and California* serve as an early prototype, but still a prototype for today's immigrants traveling to the Rocky Mountain West. Although rich and poor, young and old, city and rural residents and many others "took to the trail," many were poor farmers from the Mississippi Valley who had moved there from farther East.

Many of the Oregon Trail emigrants had no practical experience with livestock or wagons that would carry their goods for thousands of miles. Most had no knowledge of the aridity and wind of the plains, the treeless western landscape, and the high altitude and cold of the mountains. This lack of experience and preparation lead to their nickname, "greenhorns," or what today we call "rookies." Yesterday and today, these men and women of little experience made and make their share of rookie mistakes.

Now let's find out how to survive in the West in the 1840s and 1850s, and discover some clues to survival today.

Packing for the Trip

Your family of four will need well over 1,000 pounds of food for the 2,000 mile trip to Oregon, and your foodstuffs should be just the basics, including 600 pounds of flour, 120 pounds of biscuits, 400 pounds of bacon, 60 pounds of coffee, 4 pounds of tea, 100 pounds of sugar, and 200 pounds of lard. Don't forget dried fruit and vegetables, salt and pepper, yeast, and citric acid that can be added to water and prevent scurvy when your fruit and vegetables run out.

You can re-supply at the few forts along the way such as Fort Kearney, Fort Laramie, Fort Bridger, and Fort Hall, but there is no guarantee that they will have what you may need or that you will be able to afford it.

Don't forget your cooking utensils, soap, candles, extra fabric, needles and thread.

Your medicine chest may consist of quinine, blue mass, and opium. During the mid-1800s, blue mass was a widely recommended and used remedy for host of complaints including tuberculosis, constipation, toothache, depression, the pain of childbirth, syphilis, and a variety of other infections. Each pharmacist had his or her own formula including rose honey, licorice, and glycerol, but all contained mercury. If a patient took two or three pills a day, that dosage would exceed the daily limit set by today's Environmental Protection Agency by hundreds of times. Inevitably, such doses on a regular basis would lead to mercury poisoning which first causes erratic behavior and later death. Blue mass was the proverbial cure that was worse than the disease. Opium's addictive and destructive qualities limited its "medicinal" quality, too. Therefore, eliminate blue mass and opium from your medicine chest and instead stock up on brandy and whiskey.

Bring your basic tools, farm tools, a rifle, ammunition, a bowie knife, and a barrel of water on the side of the wagon. *Don't bring* your precious family heirlooms such as the grandfather clock, rocking chair, cast iron stove, or antique chest of drawers. They will take space needed for food and other essentials. Leave them with friends or family, otherwise you will have to throw them out just after the trip begins. Scavengers will be happy to pluck these treasures from the trailside.

Transportation

Of course, you and your family will need a wagon to carry your supplies and livestock to pull it. Forget the huge Conestoga wagon or "prairie schooner." It is too big and difficult to drive, and don't be tempted by the wind wagon, a cross between a wagon and sailboat. Although it can travel at fifteen miles per hour, the wind wagon always crashes. What you need is a sturdy hardwood farm wagon, a triumph of wagon technology, where the front wheels pivot and the back wheels are larger than the front ones. All of this means that the wagon turns easily, and even though the wagon bed is only four feet by ten, its big axles can support a ton of cargo.

Be sure to bring along a bucket of grease for

the wagon wheels, brake chains, drag shoes, and a spare wheel. If an axle breaks and can't be replaced, prepare to reconfigure your wagon into a two-wheeler.

If you are tempted to use horses, don't. Even if the grass is long enough, they will still need grain, and that will take precious room away from your more vital supplies. Mules can be stubborn and difficult to hitch-up, and you would need six of them plus extra grain.

Although slower, oxen are your animal of choice. They are less attractive to Indians, dependable, strong, and better able to survive on the west's sparse vegetation. You will require only four of them. If necessary, you can also eat them. In order to avoid tipping your wagon, having your team run away, or crashing into trees, practice driving your team and go easy at the beginning of the trip. You will still have 2,000 miles to go. Don't travel during the heat of the day.

Learning the Ropes

You and your family are now ready to hitch up the oxen and begin you trip to St. Louis. You are all excited. The depression in the Midwest was hurting your family and friends, and malaria and pulmonary complaints in the humid river valleys made life more tenuous.

John C. Fremont's 1843 description of the route and his handbook reassured you that the new land had much promise. Besides, men and women missionaries made the overland trip to Oregon as early as 1836, and two small parties— one in 1841, and the other in 1842, with over a hundred people, mainly families—made the journey and thrived in the Oregon country.

By mid-April, 1845, you arrive in St. Louis, and you and your family load your wagon on to a steamship. After a 200 mile trip up the Missouri River, you unload the wagon at Independence, Missouri, the most popular "jumping-off city."

You drive your team of oxen to the prairie just outside of Independence and join what looks like hundreds of emigrant campers. You make friends with some other emigrants and glean as much information as possible about the route and hazards along the way.

You discover that the large wagon trains such as the one in 1843 that included 100 wagons, 1,000 men, women, and children, and 5,000 head of cattle and oxen eventually broke up into smaller groups of family and friends. For example, some might pull off for sickness, a birth or death. Others might choose to observe the Sabbath. Rain and floods may also delay members of the wagon train, and still others may discover they just don't like the people in one smaller group and decide to join another.

You and your friends now have a chance to practice with your rifles and thereby avoid unwittingly shooting each other during the trip.

It is now approaching late April. Several hundred wagons waiting for the grass on the plains to mature have decided to break up into smaller groups of around 12 to 24 wagons. Each will depart at a specific time so that the plains grasses can be replenished after one train passes through that part of the route.

Your wagon train consists of 17 wagons and 70 people. It just elected its leaders, and it is first in the queue and ready to depart.

On the Trail

At last you are underway, and it is early May, you are surprised by the pleasant weather, plentiful grass, water, and wood. By June, the heat, wind, dryness, dust and ceaseless work take their toll on your temper and well being. Your lips are puffy and cracked, and your hands feel like sandpaper. During the first two months, you watched as two men quarreled and fought over a camping site. Another emigrant died of cholera and his wife and her fifteen year old son are now driving the wagon.

Severe thunderstorms and lighting slowed down your train and caused one team of mules to run away. They were never found, and that wagon was cut down to a hand cart. You also had a chance to regroup and rest at Fort Laramie, 667 miles from Independence, Missouri.

You are now crossing the barren alkali beds and sulfur springs that feed the Sweetwater River. Two horses mistakenly drink from the alkali beds and soon drop to the ground. Their owner has to shoot them. Fortunately, you have now come across South Pass, traversed the Green River Valley, and have just arrived at Fort Bridger— 1,070 miles from Missouri.

You are now halfway to Oregon, but you don't feel right nor does you wife. You fear the worst, cholera, even though you have been drinking only from running water. The wagon train guide looks you both in the eye and then tells you that your headaches, nausea, and dizziness stem from the high altitude, and thin air—an odd relief.

Your oxen begin to limp, and you realize that they need to be reshod. At Fort Hall on the Snake River in Idaho, you pay a farrier to reshoe them. He also sees that your wagon timbers have warped and you could lose your wheels. He sends you to a blacksmith who helps better secure your wagon. You also buy some coffee and flour. Your money is nearly gone, and you still have over 700 miles to go.

By the time you have finished shopping, the wagon train has pulled out. By nightfall you catch up, but only to find another victim of cholera, a twelve year old girl. Her parents, your friends, are distraught. After burying her, they turn back to Fort Hall. You never see or hear from them again.

The nights are getting colder, but now wood, game, and fish are plentiful. You no longer need to hunt for buffalo chips. The natural springs yield safe and fresh water. However, you still must cross the Snake River, the Boise River, and the Malheur.

When crossing the Snake, two wagons tip over and one breaks apart. The other men and their teams pull one to shore. The second wagon is lost, but the oxen break loose and swim to shore. At least something has been saved. After crossing the other two rivers, the wagon train sets up camp. Knowing that the wagon train will soon have to cross the steep Blue Mountains, the leaders call for two more days of rest.

Crossing those mountains seems like a miracle. To go up the mountain sides, several oxen teams are roped together and each wagon is pulled up, one at a time. Often an improvised winch is also necessary to aid the mountain climb. To get down a mountain and over gullies, wagons have to be lowered by ropes, one by one. At last you move down the Columbia River by ferry to the mouth of the Willamette and turn south and finally reach the fertile Willamette Valley.

Congratulations! You made it. You and your family survived. Now the new life and next "game" of survival has begun.

The Lessons for Today

So what did the American West's first survivalists teach today's outdoor adventurers? Just about everything that they knew and the lessons can be easily translated into 21st Century guides for the West's newcomers and old timers. The basic elements of survival are the same today as they were 150 years ago.

The key to survival is the will to survive. Preparation, physical fitness, a clear head, knowledge of priorities and your environment, and a willingness to improvise will help to increase your chances of surviving in the Western wilderness or its smaller towns.

What else must we possess to survive on today's westward trail? A survivor must be determined and self-directed. He or she believes that only cooperation—in contrast to pure self interest—can improve survival. He or she will know what they can change, and what they can't. If the survivors can see the prospect for change, they will fight for it. Most important, a Western survivalist will not be overcome by the challenges he or she faces. They can accept the reality of their situation, but once recognizing it, they will vigorously seek to improve it.

Our Survival

Together we have bumped along the Oregon
Trail and seen first hand how our emigrant
predecessors traveled and endured their journey
west. We have witnessed the long swath of
trail where rookie mistakes were easy. Some
were fatal or near fatal. Others were overcome.
Success was not measured in distance alone or
by hardship. It was measured by survival and
reaching their destination.

Like other Western adventurers portrayed in
this book, we have nearly reached our destination.
While I have tried to tell the truth, the trip has not
always been fun. But I hope that it has shone the
light of knowledge on the myths and then
brightened the path to a better future. I have

survived and enjoyed writing this book, and I can hope that you have survived reading it and enjoyed the trip, too.

Well prepared, clear headed, ready to improvise, and determined, I offer my survival tips and guide for life in the West—tips for newcomers and old timers, alike. Even though my guides are drawn from my life in Wyoming, they apply to any town that has an "Old West" or rural tradition. These tips can help mitigate the mistakes and misimpressions on both sides, but more importantly, they can allow us to laugh at ourselves—the true trick of survival anywhere.

The Newcomers' Survival Guide

Six years ago when my family moved from Washington, D.C., to Daniel, Wyoming, we made our share of rookie mistakes. We learned from them and are uniquely equipped to offer these tips for the West's newcomers.

When a Wyomingite says that he or she really likes your outfit, neither is referring to your clothes. They are referring to your truck.

When a Wyoming native says to woman, "nice rack" he means the antlers on a mule deer or elk, not your bosom.

Pinochle is a card game, not the story book

character whose nose grows longer whenever he tells a lie.

When a native says he or she will drag today, they don't mean drag racing or dressing in drag, but dragging their fields, which is like raking a lawn in the spring or fall, except a Wyoming drag is made from 1/4 inch steel rods linked together and pulled behind a tractor.

Get used to winter seven months a year and start planning for winter in August.

4H is not a livestock brand, but a program for kids that teaches them about ranch or farm animals and responsibility.

There is no such thing as a jackalope.

Don't wait for first run movies to come to your local movie theater or later to your video rental store. Join Netflix, and be prepared for a longer delivery time than promised in the ads.

Chinks, shotguns, and batwings don't refer to "chinks in someone's armor," bird hunting, or the wings of a bat. They refer to the different types of chaps (pronounced "shaps") worn by cowboys.

Learn to ski and snowshoe. There's not much else to do outdoors during winter.

In winter, store a shovel, tow rope, extra winter clothes, non-perishable food, water and sleeping bag in your car. You will need them.

Live year around, summer visits don't count.

Get over fresh fruit, vegetables, and fish.

When the heat and dryness of July and August hits, remember the snow, cold and wind of April and May.

Get used to the wind. It never quits.

You now live in cattle country, and a ribeye steak or any other steak should be "dirt cheap." Guess again. Two medium size ribeye steaks at your local food mart will cost eighteen dollars or more.

If you shopped at Bloomingdales, Ann Taylor, Brooks Brothers or similar stores, get accustomed to K Mart and Wal-Mart or shop online.

When driving your truck, practice the one or four finger wave with your right hand still on the steering wheel. That is the Wyoming greeting.

You will rarely find fresh fish, shrimp, or lobster. Enjoy frozen seafood.

No matter what you thought of the crowds, traffic, self importance, and wealth of your closest resort town, it now has cheaper gas, bookstores, real grocery stores, and good restaurants and that fresh fish you've been missing.

Saving the Best of the West in Wyoming

When a Wyomingite asks if you want a pop or a sack, they mean a soda and or a bag.

A burnt bag is not a paper sack singed by fire, but a cow's udder burned by the sun reflected off of the snow.

Whether the price of oil is $147 or $40 a barrel, be prepared to pay 25-35 cents more per gallon than in a major city. No old timer can tell you why and don't expect your local weekly newspaper to investigate this story—or any other story, for that matter.

During winter if you are stuck or can't see in a white-out, never leave your car or truck in a storm. The last person who did died 25 feet from her house that she could not see.

Get used to much over used ungrammatical phrases—where is your daughter *at?* I don't know where she's *at*. Where is your horse *at?* He's lost. Where is the chili cook-off *at?* I'll have to find out where it's *at*.

Don't panic if you smell something awful burning. Your house is not on fire. Your neighbor, a native Wyomingite, is simply burning his trash in a "burn barrel."

Old Timers' Survival Guide

Having worked as a cowboy and ranch hand, I can now count many "old timers" as friends. Some have shared these tips and others I have gleaned from conversations. I can now share them with you.

You can't remember the last time that you locked your front door or truck.

Waking up at 5:00 a.m. every morning is a function of getting older, not ranch work.

If you think about change too long, it will be knocking down your front door before you know it.

Saving the Best of the West in Wyoming

You are a minority. Only 4 out of 10 Wyomingites were born in Wyoming and are considered natives. The other 60% of Wyoming citizens came from someplace else, and so did your parents or grandparents.

Bask in the glory of seven month winters and blinding winds. You're used to it.

You and your horses consider mosquitoes, black flies, and horseflies "just part of nature."

If Wyoming is such a great place to live, why do almost 60% of the 18 to 24 year olds leave the state?

Imitation is the most sincere form of flattery. That is why dudes and newcomers buy cowboy boots, cowboy hats, pick-up trucks, and drink Coors or Gentleman Jack.

Hard work is a virtue, but making a profit is a necessity.

Getting bucked off your horse today hurts a lot more than it did ten years ago.

Shoeing horses is a job for younger men.

In your lifetime you will own one really good horse and stock dog.

There are too many good horses to ride a mean one.

Remind a dude or newcomer, who might work for you, that when you say ranch work begins at 6:00 a.m., you mean be there by 5:45 a.m.

If you don't know where you are, you are simply not where you want to be yet.

No matter how cold, you can never be the first to admit how cold it really is.

If you have seen -60°, you will never want to see it again.

Don't ever travel in a blizzard unless you have to feed your cows or go to the bar.

If someone really speeds by you on the road, you know that they are either from Colorado, California, or Idaho. You will mutter, "The county has just gone to hell."

When a newcomer asks you where you caught that big fish and what did you use, don't forget to say, "I caught it in that lake with a fishing rod."

Tell the newcomer or talkative ranch hand, "Pipe down, you're disturbing the quiet."

We have finally come to the end of this journey through the social life and history of Wyoming, and we have also discovered how these lessons might apply to the rest of the Rocky Mountain West. Wyoming has much to offer that is authentic and appealing. But finding and sustaining those qualities into the 21st Century will require us to dispel misleading myths and replace them with greater tolerance, respect, and social and economic diversity. These tasks will require hard work, determination, and above all a vision for Wyoming's future.

These essays have sketched a vision and started this trip to the future. But it will take newcomers and old timers alike and their children to complete this journey. I hope to see you "on the road." And don't forget that one finger wave!

Saving the Best of the West in Wyoming

Notes and Sources

State Pride

The Twin Cities population data came from a July, 2008 report by the Metropolitan Council and that data and other information on the Council can be found on its website: www.metrocouncil.org. This data was augmented by the U.S. Census Bureau's State and County Quick Facts. The information on Minnesota lakes and water quality is available on the Minnesota Pollution Control Agency's website at www.pca.state.mn.us.

Wyoming: You're So Square
(Baby I Don't Care)

The song lyrics and information on Jerry Leiber and Mike Stoller came from the Rock and Roll Hall of Fame website at www.rockhall.com The version sung by Buddy Holly is a personal favorite and has been for many years. I am also one of the many who have visited Graceland, Elvis Presley's home in Memphis, Tennessee.

The basic geography and the idea of the square state were first drawn from e-mail exchanges with John L. Allen, former professor and chair of the Geography Department at the University of Wyoming, and Larry M. Ostresh, former professor in the same department. Both are now Faculty Emeritus in the University's Geography Department. These electronic conversations were dated February 3 and 16, 2007. Other sources included Henry Gannett, *Boundaries of the United States and Several States and Territories*, Second Edition, (USGS Bulletin 171, Government Printing Office, Washington, D.C., 1900) and D.W. Meinig, *American Wests: A Preface to a Geographical Interpretation,* (Annals of American Geographers, 1972), pp 159-184.

The information on the concepts of latitude and longitude came from Dava Sobel's *Longitude: The True Story of a Lone Genius Who Solved the Greatest Scientific Problem of His Time* (New York, London, Victoria, Ontario, Auckland, Penguin Books, 1995).

The state's demographic information was drawn from the U.S. Census Bureau's *2006 American Community Survey* and its *State and County Quick Facts.* Other data came from the state's *Quick Facts: Wyoming 2007—Just the Facts,* and the NETSTATE website. The source for the wildlife data was the Wyoming Game and Fish Department's *2007 Annual Report* and the data on cattle and ranchland was drawn from the Wyoming Department of Agriculture's 2005-2006 *Annual Report* and the U.S. Department of Agriculture's National Agricultural Statistics Service's *2002 Census of Agriculture.*

The taglines or slogans for the Wyoming tourism industry, the Jackson Hole Chamber of Commerce, Sheridan, the Cowboy Shop, and Cheyenne were found on the websites of each.

The source for the real estate prices in Jackson, Wyoming, was a 2006-2007 market summary prepared by Leonard Kleiman of Sotheby's International and included as an advertising supplement in the January 16, 2008 issue of the *Jackson Hole News and Guide.*

The Equality State

The background on Wyoming's State Seal was provided by the Wyoming Secretary of State, who officially keeps the Seal, Stateline.org, and NETSTATE at www.netstate.com

The data on men and women's income and other demographic data were drawn from the U.S. Census Bureau's *2006 American Community Survey.*

Much of the information on Wyoming territorial life, the suffrage debate, and personalities, including the 1870 and 1880 Census data, were based on T.A. Larson's *History of Wyoming,* Second Edition, Revised (Lincoln and London, University of Nebraska Press, 1978), pp 64-132.

Saving the Best of the West in Wyoming

Other major sources on Wyoming Territory and the suffrage debate were the *Wyoming Blue Book, Volume One* by the Wyoming State Archives and Historical Department (Cheyenne, Wyoming, Pioneer Printing & Stationery, 1974) and the State Archive's website at http://wyoarchives.state.wy.us.

A major complement to his longer *History* was T.A. Larson's *Wyoming, A Bicentennial History* (New York, W.W. Norton and Company and the American Association for State and Local History, Nashville, 1977), pp 40-107.

The third general source was Howard R. Lamar's edition of The *New Encyclopedia of the American West,* (New Haven and London, Yale University Press, 1998).

Two important complementary sources were: A. Dudley Gardner and Verla R. Flores, *The Forgotten Frontier: A History of Wyoming Coal Mining* (Boulder, San Francisco, and London, Westview Press, 1989) and Velma Linford, *Wyoming Frontier State* (Denver, Colorado, The Old West Publishing Co., 1947).

The biographical information on James M. Ashley was provided by the Office of the Clerk, U.S. House of Representatives. Not only does the clerk's office maintain an overview of every U.S. Congress, but through the Biographical Directory of the United States Congress, or "bioguide," it has the biographical data of every member of the U.S. Congress. See http://bioguide.congress.gov.

The information on the Delaware or Lenape Indians was drawn from their website at http://www.delawaretribeofindians.nsn.us.

Beyond T.A. Larson's *History of Wyoming,* the information on Wyoming's first territorial governor, John A. Campbell, came from his *Diary 1869-1875* made available by the Wyoming State Historical Society and published in Volume 10, *the Annals of Wyoming,* January 10, 1938.

Information on Andrew Johnson and U.S. Grant was drawn from the White House website at http://www.whitehouse.gov/history/presidents, and Howard Lamar's *New Encyclopedia of the American West.*

Mark Junge's, *Wyoming: A Pictorial History* (Norfolk and Virginia Beach, The Donning Company, 1989) proved to be a useful general resource, but also aided the description of South Pass City in its early days. pp. 76-81.

Mike A. Massie's article, *Reform is Where You Find It: The Roots of Women Suffrage in Wyoming,* provided a rich, but sometimes contradictory history of the suffrage debate, including a history of Esther Hobart Morris. This article is available on the Wyoming State Archives website at http://wyoarchives.state.wy.us.

Saving the Best of the West in Wyoming

The Wyoming State Archives website also provided valuable information and research on a variety of historical topics.

The history of Wyoming women and other women homesteaders were based on Cora M. Beach's *Women of Wyoming,* (Casper, 1927); Denice Wheeler's *Feminine Frontier: Wyoming Women 1850-1900,* (Salt Lake City, 1987); Marcia Meredith Hensley's *Staking Her Claim: Women Homesteading the West,* (Glendo, Wyoming, High Plains Press, 2008); Teresa Jordan's *Cowgirls: Women of the American West,* (Garden City, New York, Anchor Press, Doubleday & Company, 1982); *Pioneer Women: The Lives of Women on the Frontier* by Linda Peavey and Ursula Smith, (Norman, Oklahoma, University of Oklahoma Press, 1996); and John Clayton's *The Cowboy Girl, the Life of Caroline Lockhart* (Lincoln and London, University of Nebraska Press, 2007).

Teva J. Scheer's *Governor Lady: The Life and Times of Nellie Tayloe Ross,* (Columbia and London, University of Missouri Press, 2005) not only provided the background on Nellie Tayloe Ross, but offered a history of other events and personalities including Ma Ferguson.

The data on Wyoming women legislators was drawn from the state legislature's website at http://legisweb.state.wy.us/2007/members, and the data on women in other legislatures came from the National Conference of State Legislatures at http://www.ncsl.org. Since the total number of members varies dramatically from state-to-state, percentages are very misleading, and that is why the comparisons are made with actual numbers.

Information on Colorado suffrage history and the first elected women state legislators came from the Colorado Archives at http://www.colorado.gov/dpa/doit/archives.

The *Readings in Wyoming History: Issues in the History of the Equality State* edited by Phil Roberts, (Laramie, Skyline West Press, 2004) provided a wide array of articles on equality in Wyoming. Particularly valuable were: *Introduction: The Organizing Concepts of Wyoming History* by Phil Roberts, *Wyoming's Estelle Reel: The First Woman Elected to a Statewide Office in America* by Sarah R. Bohl, *The Emerging Civil Rights Movement: The 1957 Wyoming Public Accommodations Statute as Case Study* by Kim Ibach and William Howard Moore, *Fired by Conscience: The Black 14 Incident at the University of Wyoming and Black Protest in the Western Athletic Conference, 1968-1970,* and *The Virginian Meets Matthew Shepard* by D. Claudia Thompson.

Wyoming's county unemployment rates were found on the Bureau of Labor Statistics' time series data on unemployment rates and employment at http.//data.bls.gov. The Economic Analysis Division of the Wyoming Department of Administration and Information provided additional information

Saving the Best of the West in Wyoming

The data on occupations was based on the Bureau of Labor Statistics May, 2007, State Occupational Employment and Wage Estimates: Wyoming at http://www.bls.gov.

The policy prescriptions for improving the economic life of Wyoming women were based on the Best Practices Library of the National Governors' Association at http://www.nga.org.

The information on Wyoming Indians and casino gambling were based on reports and a detailed chronology of the events available in the *Casper-Star Tribune* Archives at www.casperstartribune.net or at trib.com. The Indian Gaming Association also provided information on the background of state compacts and the economic impact of the Indian gaming at http://www.indiangaming.org.

The information on Matthew Shepard and his case also came from a University of Wyoming detailed chronology of events at http://uwacadweb.uwyo.edu and ABC news coverage at http://abcnews.go.com/2020/story.

Place Names

The history of Thomas Fitzpatrick was based on Robert M. Utley's *A Life Wild and Perilous; Mountain Men and the Paths to the Pacific,* (New York, Henry Holt and Company) Leroy Haffen, *Broken Hand: The Life and Times of Thomas*

Fitzpatrick, Mountain Man, Guide, and Indian Agent (Denver, Colorado, Old West Publishing, 1931); and Howard R. Lamar, ed., *The New Encyclopedia of the American West*, (New Haven and London, Yale University Press, 1998).

As noted in the text the source of the same place names outside of Wyoming was the U.S. Geologic Survey's Name Information System and found at geonames.usgs.gov.

Odds and Ends

The data on Wyoming land ownership came from *Wyoming 2007—Just the Facts.* The information on the Wyoming Landscape Conservation Initiative came from the USGS website, http://pubs.usgs.gov/sir/2008/5073/.

The citation of the *Science* article was based on an article in the *Washington Post,* February 11-17, 2008, entitled "Meltdown in the West" and written by Marc Kaufman, p 33.

The study on the impact of global warming on Yellowstone National Park by Stanford University scientist Sarah McMenamin was cited in an October 28, 2008 *USA Today* article by Doyle Rice, "Warming affecting Walden, Yellowstone," found on page 9D.

The information on the EPA's Appeals Board action on the Vernal, Utah coal-fired power plant was reported in the November 14, 2008 issue of *USA Today.* The reporter was Paul Davidson and the article, "Coal power plants may have to clean up their act," was placed on page 2B.

The information about Steve Gray, the state climatologist, and the impact of global warming on Wyoming was based on a September 23, 2008 *Casper Star Tribune* article by Phil White, "Scientists: Global Warming seriously affects Wyoming."

The information on the Wyoming land trusts came from the Land Trust Alliance and websites of each of the noted land trusts. Any search engine can locate these sites.

The information on EnCana was first based on Paul Jensen, *Hard and Noble Lives: a Living Tradition of Cowboys and Ranchers in Wyoming's Hoback Basin,* (Pronghorn Press, 2007), pp 317-350.

The data on the Jonah Interagency Office's conservation easements came from their website and updated reports, e-mails, and conversations with habitat biologist, Dan Stroud.

The report on the EPA's review of BLM draft EIS was based on a *Jackson Hole News and Guide* article, "EPA Slams New Plan for Sublette Gas Field," February 20, 2008, by Cory Hatch. The data on ozone levels was drawn from Pinedale Online, published on the days of the alerts at pinedaleonline.com.

The information on the Wyoming Wildlife and Natural Resource Trust was based on its website at http://wwnrt.state.wy.us. and the *Casper Tribune* website and Archives at trib.com.

Similarly, the information on the Wildlife Heritage Foundation of Wyoming was based on its website at http://www.whgfw.org.

The information and data on the sage grouse were drawn from the downloaded reports of the Wyoming Game and Fish Department and the USGS, and each was identified in the text.

The *Atlanta Journal Constitution* provided the background on Michael Vick, and the source of the Wyoming dog fighting debate and legislative action was the *Casper Star Tribune* at trib.com

Information on the Wyoming legislative drunk driving debates was drawn from the *Casper Star Tribune Archives* including the open container debate reported on February 23, 2007 and the 2008 discussion of stiffer DUI penalties on February 22, 2008.

The statistics on drunk driving came from the Department of Transportation's National Highway Transportation Safety Administration and its data series on Fatalities and Fatality Rates 1994-2006 at http://www.fars.nhtsa.dot.gov. Other important data and current DUI laws came from Stateline.org, Mothers Against Drunk Driving at http://www.madd.org, the National Conference of State Legislatures at http://www.ncsl.org, Alcohol Alert at http://www.alcoholalert.com. and United States DUI laws at http://www.duidrivinglaws. The last source of data on Wyoming alcohol related arrests came from the November, 2008, study, Evaluation of Alcohol Factors in Custodial Arrests in the State of Wyoming 2008, by The

Saving the Best of the West in Wyoming

Wyoming Association of Sheriffs and Police Chiefs. The information of Wyoming's new law requiring ignition interlocks for repeat offenders and certain first offenders was reported by Marjorie Korn on the front page of the March 4, 2009 edition of the *Casper Star Tribune,* and the article was entitled "Final DUI bill passes."

The health data was drawn from the Center for Disease Controls' 2007 publication, *Chronic Diseases: The Leading Causes of Death in Wyoming* (and the United States), and its publication, the *Ten Leading Causes of Death and Comparisons by State, 2004.*

The CDC's trend data for Wyoming and others states were pulled from its Behavior Risk Factor Surveillance System, its National Vital Statistics System, and its Heart Disease Facts and Statistics. Also stateline.org provided valuable state by state comparisons.

The data on suicides came from the CDC's WISQARS website "Fatal Injury Reports" and the American Association of Suicidology. The health data on Wyoming Indian tribes came from the U.S. Bureau's 2006 American Community Survey

Newcomers and Old Timers

Beyond T.A. Larson's History of Wyoming, my primary historical source was Gordon Olaf Hendrickson, ed., *Peopling the High Plains: Wyoming's European Heritage,* (Cheyenne, Wyoming State Archives and Historical Department, 1977).

Since immigration and ethnicity are under valued topics among Wyoming researchers, this book remains the best study of European immigration. This dilemma was addressed by Carl V. Hallberg in his article, "Ethnicity in Wyoming," one of the many articles included in *Readings of Wyoming: Issues in the History of the Equality State*, Phil Roberts, ed., (Laramie, Skyline West Press, 2004).

The two other historical sources include A. Dudley Gardner and Verla R. Flores, *The Forgotten Frontier: A History of Wyoming Coal Mining*, (Boulder, San Francisco, and London, Westview Press, 1989) and Howard R. Lamar's *New Encyclopedia of the American West*, (New Haven and London, Yale University Press, 1998).

Walter Prescott Webb's *The Great Plains*, (Lincoln and London, University of Nebraska Press, Bison Book, 1981) provided typically informative insight into western settlement.

The current immigration data was drawn from the U.S. Census Bureau's 2006 *American Community Survey*, its *American FactFinder*, the Wyoming Economic Analysis Division's *Annual Population Estimates from 2000-2006*, the Wyoming Housing Database Partnership *Final Report August 28, 2007*, and the Wyoming Department of Employment's Research and Planning Division's 2006 report, *States of Origin for Wyoming Workers*.

Saving the Best of the West in Wyoming

Struthers Burt's *Powder River Let'er Buck*, (New York and Toronto, Farrar & Rinehart, 1938), provided a useful background to Wyoming settlement and the British ranchers who settled in the Powder River Basin.

Lawrence M. Wood's *British Gentlemen in the Wild West: The Era of the Intensely English Cowboy*, (New York and London, the Free Press, 1989), gave additional insight into British cowboy life in the American West.

Edited by Michael McCoy, *Classic Cowboy Stories: 18 Extraordinary Tale of the Old West*, (New York, MJF Books, 2004), offered another perspective on the Wyoming cowboy.

Charles M. Russell's *Rawhide Rawlins Stories*, (Pasadena, California, Trails End Publishing, 1946), gave an interesting insight into that character and his stories.

Robert G. Athearn's *The Mythic West In the Twentieth-Century American*, (Lawrence, Kansas, University Press of Kansas, 1986) gave very keen insight into the real and mythical West and how they merge.

The quote on the nature of myth by Thomas Keneally came from *Schindler's List*, (New York, Simon & Schuster, 1982), p. 232.

Are the Times A Changing?

The history of Wyoming's economy was based on T.A. Larson's *History of Wyoming*, Second Edition, Revised (Lincoln and London, University of Nebraska Press, 1978), pp. 163-194 and T.A. Larson's Wyoming, *A Bicentennial History* (New York, W.W Norton and Company and the American Association of State and Local History, Nashville, 1977), pp 143-185.

The current and historical data on Wyoming agriculture was drawn from the Wyoming Department of Agriculture's *2005-2006 Annual Report* and the U.S. Department of Agriculture's National Agricultural Statistics Service's *2002 Census of Agriculture.*

The term, *cowboy economics*, was coined by Harold L. Oppenheimer in *Cowboy Economics: Rural Land as an Investment* (Interstate Printers and Publishers, Danville, Illinois, 1966).

The initial data on the national and state Gross Domestic Product by industry, employment by industry, the state's revenue sources, and the diversification index came from *Wyoming's Economic Insight and Outlook*, April 23, 2008 by Wenlin Liu, Senior Economist, Economic Analysis Division, State of Wyoming.

Other sources were *Wyoming Economic Outlook*, April 13, 2007 by Buck McVeigh, Administrator of the Economic Analysis Division, the State of Wyoming; and *A Socioeconomic Profile*

Saving the Best of the West in Wyoming

of Wyoming by Headwaters Economics, December 4, 2007. However, most of this data was based on the U.S. Department of Commerce's Bureau of Economic Analysis and its Regional Economic Accounts' data series. Its data series, *SA25N*, provides information on Wyoming's full-time and part-time employment by NAICS industry. Similarly series *SA05N* gives the information on personal income by major source and earning's by NAICS industries.

A 2001-2007 time series on personal income and earnings by industry based on BEA data was also available from the state's Economic Analysis Division's Website.

The information on the state's energy picture came from the state's *Quick Facts Wyoming 2007-2008, Just the Facts*; The American Wind Energy Association at http://www.awea.org/projects/, *T. Boone Pickens' Wind Vision* at http://www.pickensdplan.com/theplan,the Federal Energy Information Administration at http:/www.eia.doe.gov; and "Billionaires Bank on Wyo Wind," by Dustin Bleizeffer, *Casper Star Tribune*, July 31, 2008.

The information on GE, the University of Wyoming, IGCC technology, and GE's ecomagination program was based on a GE new release, *GE signs Letter of Intent with University of Wyoming to Develop New Coal Gasification Technology*, February, 13, 2008, and GE's 2006 ecomagination report, *Delivering on Ecomagination.*

Additional information on the cooperative agreement between The University of Wyoming and GE Energy came from a page 1, October 31, 2008, *Casper Star Tribune* story by Dustin Bleizeffer, "UW, GE Coal-Gasification Deal Moves Forward."

The information on the carbon dioxide capture project was widely reported in Wyoming and Montana, but my source was an AP story run on page 8 in the *Jackson Hole Daily News* on November 19, 2008.

The economic data on travel and tourism in Wyoming came from *The Economic Impact of Travel on Wyoming; 1997-2006 Detailed State and County Estimates* prepared for the State Office of Travel and Tourism, Wyoming Business Council by Dean Runyan Associates, September,2007.

The National Park visitation numbers were prepared by the National Park Service's Public Use Statistics Office at http://www.nature.nps.gov/stats/viewReport.cfm.

The data and report from the U.S. Department of Agriculture's Economic Research Service came from *Rural America At A Glance*, 2007 Edition, *Economic Information Bulletin 31*, October, 2007. Similar data was cited in the 2009 Colorado College *State of the Rockies Report Card*, pp.52-61.

The 2007 poll on Wyoming Public Opinion on Natural Resource Conservation and Development is cited in the text. However, a copy of the poll and more information can be obtained by calling the University of Wyoming at 307-766-5080 or accessing this website www.uwyo.edu/openspaces.

The May, 2009 poll came from the report, *Building the Wyoming We Want: Priorities and Values Study*, by Dee Allsop of Heart + Mind Strategies.

The study by Kara Grau, *The Changing Structure of Montana's Economy; What Is Tourism's Place?* was conducted for the Institute for Tourism and Recreation Research, College of Forestry and Conservation, University of Montana, Missoula, MT, July, 2007.

Background on Wyoming politics was provided by Larry Hubbell, Editor, *The Equality State: Government and Politics in Wyoming*, Fifth Edition (Eddie Bowers publishing, Peosta, Iowa, 2004).

The state and county registration and voting performance numbers were available from the Secretary of State's Website at http://soswy.state.us/election.
County Clerks in the key counties also graciously provided up-to-date 2008 registration numbers and the 2002 numbers.

The information on Americans' ambivalence about the federal government was based on Albert H. Cantril and Susan Davis Cantril's *Reading Mixed Signals: Ambivalence in American Public*

Opinion about Government, Woodrow Wilson Center Press, Washington, D.C., 1999).

A Survivor's Guide to Living in the West

John Mack Faragher's *Women and Men on the Overland Trail*, Second Edition, (New Haven and London, Yale Nota Bene, Yale University Press, 2001) served as a primary source for the history and travel on the Oregon Trail.

W.J. Ghent's *The Road to Oregon* (New York, AMS Press, 1929) was just as valuable a source as John Mack Faragher's book.

Jacqueline Morley's *How Would You Survive in the American West?* (New York, London, Hong Kong, Sydney. Danbury, Connecticut, Franklin Watts, 1995) provided a wonderful and easily accessible travelogue of the Oregon Trail.

Howard Lamar's *New Encyclopedia of the American West*, (New Haven and London, Yale University Press, 1998) offered additional background on the Oregon Trail.

The website, *The Oregon Trail*, built by teachers, Mike Trinklein and Steve Boettcher, creators of *The Oregon Trail*, a documentary aired by PBS, was an exceptionally valuable source of information, particularly the full text archival documents including emigrant diaries and memoirs. The site is

Saving the Best of the West in Wyoming

http://www.isu.edu/~trinmich/introduction.html

Gregory J. Davenport's *Wilderness Survival* (Mechanicsburg, Pennsylvania, Stackpole Books, 1998) served as one source for information on survival tips.

Larry Dean Olsen's *Outdoor Survival Skills*, Provo, Utah, Brigham Young University Press, 1973) was the second source on outdoor survival.

Appendix

2002 Gubernatorial Election

	Freudenthal	Dawson	Bebout
Albany	6,772	205	4,404
Carbon	3,493	148	2,345
Laramie	18,563	385	11,487
Natrona	13,175	610	9,825
Sweetwater	7,808	328	5,206
Teton	4,281	155	3,128
Converse	2,092	98	2,281
Fremont	5,500	258	8,108
Hot Springs	1,212	27	942
Platte	2,122	101	1,645
Sheridan	5,510	189	5,567

2006 U.S. House Election

	Trauner	Cubin
Albany	7,350	4,133
Carbon	2,769	2,634
Laramie	18,188	11,869
Natrona	13,848	10,793
Sweetwater	6,648	5,532
Teton	6,218	2,598
Converse	2,170	2,264
Fremont	6,610	6,541
Hot Springs	999	1,160
Platte	1,842	1,967
Sheridan	5,255	5,883

Breinigsville, PA USA
02 November 2009
226794BV00002B/1/P

9 781932 636581